Best Stud

Volume 4

Winners of the 1998
KENNEDY CENTER AMERICAN COLLEGE THEATER FESTIVAL
One-Act Play Competition

The Kennedy Center

THE JOHN F. KENNEDY CENTER FOR THE PERFORMING ARTS
WASHINGTON, DC 20566-0001

James A. Johnson, Chairman
Lawrence J. Wilker, President
Derek E. Gordon, Vice President, Education

Edited
by Lauren Friesen
University of Michigan-Flint

Dramatic Publishing

Woodstock, Illinois • England • Australia • New Zealand

Contents

Introduction

The publication of volume 4 of *Best Student One Acts* by Dramatic Publishing marks a new beginning for this series. The three previous editions were published under the auspices of the Kennedy Center and the American College Theatre Festival. The plays in these four volumes are all winners in regional competitions sponsored by the American College Theatre Festival. Prior to the publication of this series, the winning one-act plays received very little recognition unless they were selected for performance at the Kennedy Center.

The Kennedy Center/American College Theatre Festival's Michael Kanin Playwriting Awards Program began in 1974. The list of national winners contains a number of notable playwrights including Pulitzer Prize-winning playwright Paula Vogel who won the 1977 national competition with *Meg*; Lee Blessing with *The Authentic Life of Billy the Kid*; and James Leonard Jr., with *The Diviners*. These names are now associated with the vibrant and divergent world of contemporary theatre.

Whereas the national winners have received considerable attention, the regional winners were largely ignored for many years. As a result, many significant works were unavailable for additional exposure. Maybe the most glaring example of a play which won a regional award but not the national is George C. Wolfe's *Up for Grabs*. The publication of volume 1 in this series of Best Student One Acts altered the landscape for the students who won their regional competitions. The initial vision for these anthologies came from Jeffery Scott Elwell, who also edited the first volume, with the endorsement and support from the Michael Kanin Playwriting Awards Committee. This anthology series then emerged from the efforts of Harlene Marley, chair of that committee, to put the vision into action. Dramatic Publishing's release of this and future editions marks a significant departure from the previous volumes. The publishing idea that germinated a number of years ago has now reached full maturity with the assistance of a major publishing house.

The publication of this series is one small effort to bring new works to the attention of interested directors, actors, playwrights and scholars. The variety of institutions represented in the series is significant in a national publication. The 32 playwrights represent 24 different schools located in 21 states. This anthology is in fact the only nationwide publication for student playwrights because it includes plays from the eight national regions within the American College Theatre Festival. The size and nature of the theatre program varies greatly. Some of the authors are undergraduate students from colleges in small-town America while others are pursuing graduate degrees at large, urban universities.

Geography alone is not the only means by which difference can be observed. The sense of a national portraiture is also reflected in the diversity of subject matter. These plays explore themes from a variety of ethnic, religious and social perspectives. Included are history plays, autobiographical explorations, poetic worlds and styles that include an example from nearly every age in theatre history. There are overtones of tragedy, surrealism, comedy, farce, epic and so forth. The value of each work is not limited to its command of form and style. Instead, each play opens another window on American identity from the perspective of a student playwright. Some playwrights open that window to a tragic landscape, while others show us humor, absurdity, or pathos that is rooted in careful observation. Each work reflects a desire to participate in the process of creating a work of art that is an expression to a unique voice. Some of those voices shout from housetops, whereas others explore the hidden chambers of the soul. The assortment of themes, styles and values reflected in these works serves as a mirror to the diversity of America's academic institutions and society itself.

Each play represents a personal journey from the blank page to the stage while also symbolically representing a narrative larger than the play itself. Actors, directors, designers, classmates and supportive faculty from many institutions have guided these playwrights to this stage of development. These collaborative teams deserve commendation and gratitude for their willingness to work with original plays.

This volume represents one dimension of the Kennedy Center's multifaceted initiative for student playwrights. The Michael Kanin Playwriting Awards Program sponsors a variety of national student playwriting awards. Some include publication for the winning playwright and an opportunity for the playwright to participate in play development workshops. The Jean Kennedy Smith Award is given for the best play on the theme of disability. For the best play on World Peace and Disarmament, the Fourth Freedom Foundation provides first- and second-place awards. Anchorage Press offers the Theatre for Youth Playwriting Award. Dramatic Publishing will continue to publish the

Lorraine Hansberry Award for the best play that explores African or African-American themes, and will be publishing several awards recently established, including: The David Mark Cohen Playwriting Award, open to all playwrights; the National AIDS Fund/CFDA-Vogue Initiative Award for the best play that deals with AIDS/HIV; The Mark Twain Comedy Playwriting Award; and the Sí TV Playwriting Award, created to stimulate the voices of young Latino playwrights in America. The John Cauble Award is given for the best student short play. The Musical Theatre Award is available to student lyricists, composers or book authors. The workshop opportunities for the winning playwrights include Sundance Theatre Laboratory, the Bay Area Playwrights Festival, and the Kennedy Center for the Performing Arts.

These anthologies could not exist without the untold hours that regional playwriting committee chairs have devoted to developing original plays within each region. Regional chairs Kate Snodgrass, Garry Garrison, Steve Sarratore, Jim Epperson, Clyde Ruffin, Ray Paolino, Bryan Willis and Judith Royer have assisted with the development and implementation of this volume while also serving as a guide and advocate for the other playwriting awards. I also wish to express my gratitude to Jeffery Scott Elwell for his initial vision for the series, to Harlene Marley for unwavering advocacy for student playwrights, to Kenneth Robbins for his commitment to award and publication venues for student plays, to Jeff Koep for his support in sustaining and developing the programs within the Playwriting Award Committee, to Derek Gordon and his innovative leadership at the Kennedy Center, to John Lion and his discerning eye for new plays and playwriting opportunities, and to Susan Shaffer and her effective management of American College Theatre Festival. Finally, I want to thank my colleagues at the University of Michigan-Flint for their assistance and encouragement. The theatre department, under the guidance of Carolyn Gillespie, has demonstrated an exceptional level of commitment to student playwriting and creative theatrical ventures.

I am grateful for the opportunity to serve as editor of this volume.

ALTER EGOS
So Many Characters. So Little Time.

Jon McGovern
New York University

ALTER EGOS
So Many Characters. So Little Time.

PRE-SHOW: The stage empty except for a coat stand in a small pool of light. It is covered in various shirts and jackets and bags and props—the things of Alter Egos waiting to be brought to life.

THE IMPORTANCE OF BEING ZARZUFFA

(Pumping Arabic Techno music plays and disco lights flash as Zarzuffa, the "randomly foreign" pampered, arrogant and completely fabulous playboy, runs in through the audience and onto the stage wearing a designer outfit (with huge designer logos all over it), sunglasses and carrying a cell phone. He strikes a pose center stage, with his back to the audience. The front of the stage lights up like a fashion runway and he turns and works it—checking out the audience, sneering, growling, cooing, then jumps to the center of the stage.)

Everyone stop what you're doing!
(Lights flash up to full and music stops.)
Stop your eating! Stop your drinking! Stop your petty conversations! I am here, the one you want to see, the one you want to talk about, the one you want to be! So now that I am here...go ahead eat, drink, dance be merry...come on! PARTY!
(Sings.)
Be my lover! Be my lover! Be my lover! Lover! Lover!

(Stops, sees an audience member.)

Oh, hello...we have not met yet, my name is Zarzuffa. Don't be fooled, I'm not trying to pick you up, it's just my accent, it makes everything sound sexy! Do you like my outfit? It costs more than your apartment... D&G, Gucci, Armani, Versace, Prada...retail price $15,000. You know why? Because of the *logos*. I only wear clothes with gigantic designer logos on them! It lets you know they're expensive—if I could wear a price tag, I would! But...I can afford it, my father is richer than...well...than *God!* Ha ha! It's true though, ah, it's true! He sent me here to America to get a good western education—you know at first I say No! No! No! Zarzuffa says NO! But then—I come here, I go to disco dancing, go to Gucci store, get my limo, see beautiful American women... I say, Yes! Yes! I never want to go back... Never! Never! Never! Zarzuffa says NEVER!

(Reconsidering.)

Well, maybe to Europe—once I conquer all of U.S.A., I go to Europe. But, oh no, I know what your thinking, then America will become slow and boring. People will say "Zarzuffa! Zarzuffa—where are you? Oh Zarzuffa! Zuffa, Zoofy, oh my Zarzuffini!"

(Pauses his feigned crying, looks at audience, smiles.)

Ah...Don't worry, U.S.A.! I only take one class a semester, so it will take me at least ten years to get my degree. Yes! There are so many other things to do—shopping for clothes, going to bars and going to workout! I belong to ten health clubs. That's ten personal trainers! Two hundred fifty dollars an hour each! Five times a week! You do the math... I must work for the perfect body: #1 legs, #1 chest, #1 abs, #1 butt, #1 biceps...

(Looks at biceps.)

Well, maybe not yet #1 biceps. Maybe one point five or #2... But never mind! Zarzuffa is number one at so many things... I don't want to hog them all! But I must look good, for I am looking for a wife. My father has told me if I want to rule the family empire, I must have a wife. He told me if I do not have a wife before I am thirty he will cut me off.

(Looks around, confiding in the audience.)

I am 29 and three-quarters right now! He says to me, "Enough sowing your oats!" I say, "Zarzuffa is a wild stallion, he must sow oats!" He says, "No money for you without a wife" I say, "Yes, Father." So, now I need a woman! But she is hard to find! She must be perfect. She must be—by ancient family law: stylish—to decorate our mansions, gorgeous—to make all other men drool with envy, tall—to make sure our children can be supermodels, smart—to run the empire with me, ambitious—to crush other empires, and blonde—just a personal fetish. But, oh I look and look and look, but I do not find her—I try out thousands of women which I enjoy, but it is labor-intensive! And also so many almost fit but something is wrong—too tall, not blonde, not smart, cannot wear stiletto heels, too much flatulence.

(Cell phone rings, he answers it.)

Hello? Yes, I'll be there at nine o'clock, I'll pick you up, I can't talk now, I am talkin' to people...

(Looks to audience.)

I'm talkin' to you...

(Getting angrier.)

Look! I'll be there! Nine o'clock!

(To audience.)

Excuse me one moment...

(Turns away, starts raging in a broken, foreign dialect.)
Asanseer mishkyaiss! Ya habrr be arabaya khalas!! Allah!
Ill mish khedda! Iowa asanseer ya beek! I'll be there!
Don't talk to me that way! I am Zarzuffa! Don't talk to
Zarzuffa that way! I am Zarzuffa! Zarzuffa!

*(Disconnects the line and turns to audience, again a
charmer.)*
Sorry 'bout that... But speaking of the phone... If you
know anyone who could be my wife please tell them to
call my 1-900 number! It's 2.99 per minute—a small in-
vestment in what could lead to so much more. Please tell
them to call 1-900-ZARZUFFA-I-WANT-TO-BE-YOUR-
QUEEN. I wanted to call it 1-900-ZARZUFFA-I-WANT-
TO-BE-YOUR-QUEEN-you-hot-burning-stud-of-love-I-c
an't-get-enough-of-your-love-oh-Zarzuffazarzuffazarzuffa
—but they say it is too long. I also put ads in newspaper,
magazines, billboards, my God...even skywriting!! For I
must find MY QUEEN!! *(Blackout.)*

*(Old-time gospel music plays as The Actor goes back to
the coat stand, transforms into Aunt Bertha. She wears
reading glasses and a lacy white shawl as she calls out
to one of her "kids.")*

AUNT BERTHA'S LE PETITE PROBLEM

*(Entering—calling offstage to a child who doesn't seem
to be able to finish his goodbye.)*

Now, Lamar—you hold your brother's hand, you hear? All
right! Oh-oh-oh-OK. All right! Al-oh-all-ri-oo-oh-oh-OK!!

All right! Bye, buh-bye buh-bye bye bye baby— You tell your mama Aunt Bertha said hi! Buh-bye bye bye OK yes kissy kiss OK all right bye bye bye bye.

(Sits in her chair.)

Lord, I hope that child doesn't grow up to be a freak...

(Sighs, then notices the audience.)

Oh! Hiiiii! Y'all are sorta new around here, right? 'Cause I know everybody...

(Puts on her glasses and checks out the audience.)

Hmmmmmm. Hmm. Hmm. Hmm. Hmm. Hm. Hm. Hmm. Well...I'm Aunt Bertha! Oh, everybody calls me that! 'Cept my husband, Earl, he calls me baby—and that's the way I like it! Unless he gets that ova-fifty husband disease.

(To audience member.)

You know the one I mean, girl—when his butt gets glued to the chair and he wants me to get him somethin', then he calls me—"Berth-AAAA!"

(Lets out her Aunt Bertha-cackle.)

You get it?

(Still laughing.)

He's sittin', and the chair...BERTHAAA!!

(More Aunt Bertha cackling.)

Oh, but seriously, child, I like it when people call me *Aunt* Bertha. Ya know... I did have some people come around here once and say, "Bertha! Ya can't let people keep callin' you *Aunt* Bertha, that makes people think of *Aunt* Jemimah, and that sets us back thirty years!" I thought about that...but, hell, I'm not on a syrup bottle, I don't have a rag tied around my head and I'm certainly not servin' up pancakes to the world! I just like *Aunt* Bertha. It's more familiar—it's mainly for the neighborhood kids.

Makes 'em feel more comfortable. Makes 'em feel like they got an auntie watching out for them. I like watching folks,

(To audience member.)

not in the dirty, video kinda way! You naughty!! But seeing the goings on— Oh! I watch kids, babies, mothers, fathers, uncles, aunts, pregnant girls who drop out of school, hoes cheatin' on their men, punks in leather who turn out to be drag queens—you know, regular folks. I give advice, too. Good advice. The people who take my advice— Weeeeeell...things always turn out all right for them. That's usually the people on my side of the street who I'm closer to—who know me.

(Pause.)

The people who don't take my advice, usually the people on the other side of the street, weeeeellll, they end up on daytime trash TV. Really, chile, sometimes it's like looking across the street at the *TV Guide*! Like...Oooh! Kanita on *Ricki* at one, FaNita on *Montel* at two, BaSita on *Sally Jessy* at three, Manifa on *Jerry Springer* at four, hell, even Missy Thang Lontresse at the end of the street on *Oprah* at five. You know I always thought I should have my own talk show—*The Aunt Bertha Show*—ooooohhh—it would be beautiful! I wouldn't have one of those synthesizer theme songs like everybody else... NO, I'd have Linette from church belt out "Bertha's Theme" while my cousin Kiki played the B-3 organ and I would do the Aunt Bertha dance.

(She jumps up doing a funky hands-in-the-air dance, a cross between getting the spirit in church, Saturday night fever and the roboto, while singing.)

Here comes Aunt Bertha! Hey! Hey! Here comes Aunt Bertha! Hey! Hey! Oooooooooh!! I'd do it every week until it became a national craze like the macarena or the twist or oooh like my favorite—the electric slide!

(Does the electric slide.)

Huh! It's electric! Huh!! Aunt Bertha!

(Cackles.)

Oh, I'd get all the good topics too—

(Pointing to a different audience member with each topic.)

How to keep a man, how to keep a woman, how to cook a spicy corn bread chicken, in-depth study on how to achieve peace in Guatemala, gossip 'bout the stars, the cost of nuclear missile disarmament—but most of all— how to be happy with who you are and love yo'self! I'm just plain ol' sick of those fashion magazines—*Vogue* and *W*, and...Hoochies ago-go...and those runway models for Gucci and Calvin and Latiesha-whoever, lookin' all anorexic, forcin' some beautiful, big-boned, full-figured women to feel bad about themselves!!

(Pause, then seriously.)

Now...I'm a big woman. I've always been a big woman! My mama, granmama, great-granmama and probably my ancestors aaalll the way back in Cleveland...were big women too, and I know they were some hot mamas! Shakin' it here, shakin' it there, lookin' good bein' our size! None of that starvin' yo'self.

(To audience member.)

You hear me, girl? Eat what you like—love yo'self! That's the motto for my restaurant! AUNT BERTHA'S FAT-ASS CAFE! I was sick of people usin' fat ass as a negative—so when I opened the cafe I figured I'd take away its power—so FAT ASS it is. You know, I did try to think of other terms—Voluptuous Behind, Large Bottom, Comfy Seat Cafe, but, honey, FAT ASS says it all—with pride!

(Getting up.)

Girl! Boy! if you got a fat ass, show it off! Wear a bikini—show it to the world! Touch it! Rub it around! Let it roll around in the wind! If you need to hop a flight to Brazil, for Carnivaal, wearin' a hot pink g-string and get up on the float and go...

(Moves into a rhythmic shake.)

Boom-bida-boom-bida—I like my ass—Boom-biba-boom-bida—I like my ass!

(Stops.)

You do whatchu gotta do! That's what makes me mad! All these skinny-ass people tryin' to dictate what's pretty and what's not and what people gotta eat and not eat. For example what's goin' on now! It's those Le Petit Cafe people—oooh they make me so mad! Whoo! I'm gettin' hot just thinkin' about it!

(Fans herself.)

You know, at Aunt Bertha's we serve collard greens with bacon, home fries, chitlins, all the good rich stuff! Everybody in my neighborhood eats there and loves it. We've been a great success! But you know, where there's success and money there's jealousy...so the bigwigs at a chain of so-called "health food" restaurants called Le Petite Cafe aka skinny-ass cafe—where their specialty is celery—let me tell you I don't remember celery ever curin' any colds like some chicken and dumplin' soup!

(To audience member.)

Do you, girl? Me neitha! Well, they heard about my success and thought of the dollars they could make by exploiting everybody's fear of fat! They decided to come into my neighborhood—which is fine, variety is good—but they started a negative ad campaign against my restaurant! Put up all these signs sayin' things like, "'Tis the season to get chubby—so don't...eat at Aunt Bertha's..."

(Pause, she realizes something is not quite right about that.)

...or somethin' like that! All I know is, they rhyme, there are a lot of them, and they made me mad! And ya know, I still don't know what to do! They're still up there! I tried to talk to them, but Monsieur Petite wouldn't even take my calls! I thought about law suits, you know, 1-800 L-A-W-Y-E-R and things like that, but that will take forever...

(In jest.)

You know if I had my *Aunt Bertha Show*, I could call up some publicity, start a debate and can a public apology fast as can be!

(Pause.)

OOOooooh. OOOOOh. Oooh. Oooh. OoooooooOh. That's a good idea! On the cable channel...right after BET...is a public access channel and Jamal, Linette's son, works there! He could get me on...and I could star the real... one-time only...VERY SPECIAL EPISODE OF...THE AUNT BERTHA SHOW! *(Blackout.)*

(Girlie country music plays as The Actor returns to the coat stand and removes Bertha and straightens up, the hips jut out, hand on the hip...puts on a red-and-white checked Daisy Dukes-style shirt, tied at the waist, grabs a big ugly handbag with a sunflower on it and poses in pure wannabe glamour style as Lerlene.)

LERLENE ESCAPES THE BUBBAS

(Lights flash up as she turns and runs breathlessly downstage.)

Ohmigod! I just had this—*epiphany*—I think that's the word —it was like a flash of just knowin'—I had to get out! So, I just ran out of my trailer fast as I could—I only took my Merry-go-Round handbag and my two little dogs. I had to get out! The Bubbas were drivin' me crazy! When I say the Bubbas I mean my boyfriend Bubba and his two kids.

(Pause as the emotion builds inside of her.)

Bubba

(On the pouty verge of tears.)

and Bubba—the man named his two sons the same thing—which woulda been fine if they hadn't been twins! Oh those kids! Always wantin' somethin'—attention... Food! Water! I can't be bothered with that—especially not durin' my soap-opera slash talk-show hours! First of all...

(Her voice moves into her seductive range.)

I'm gonna be an actress. So soap operas are like crucial actin' lessons for me...

(A sudden switch back to the loud Lerlene we've met before.)

...and, second, I need to see the talk shows 'cause sometimes that's the only way I get to see my family! I mean, last week I missed my cousins BaSita and FaNita on *Jerry Springer!* Anyway, the main reason I left is...'cause... well...

(Does a Wonder Woman-style twirl.)

I'm gon' be famous! ...a supermodel/singer/actress—triple threat! and I need to be in a situation with a man who is going to support me in my career! 'Cause I'm on my way...I'm in training, I practice like, um, runway walkin' here in the trailer park...it's like...watch...

(Runs upstage and strikes her starting pose, then begins to walk.)

One-two-work-bitch one-two and look and look and look and look... I do *Vogue* covers, it's like...chick chick

(She poses.)

Chick chick

(Another awful pose halfway between a cheerleading pose and a porno still.)

I'm ready...ready to be...discovered.

(She throws one hand in the air in a glamourous pose, but then breaks down.)

But Bubba, Bubba and Bubba didn't want to let me go! Old Bubba just wanted us to get married and for me to get fat and pregnant! Now first of all, if I'm gonna be a super-model I can't be fat, I gotta make sure to stay thin. I sometimes eat nuthin' but Slim Fast for days—fried Slim Fast, Slim Fast fricassee, baked Slim Fast, Slim Fast ice cream, Slim Fast muffins—you know, 'cause I know that Naomi Campbell don't have no cellulite so I better not neither!

(Slaps her butt.)

I work out too! I don't have 'nuff money to join no gym so I do my workout anywhere I can. I love doing that Stairmaster but I can't get on them big-ass machines, so I just do the low-cost Stairmaster. I go to a really tall building and I just run up and down the stairs...

(Starts feigning her workout.)

...till I've burned at least a thousand calories and then I just drop!

(Falls dramatically to the ground.)

Then I just hope that some cute businessman or security guard will call me an ambulance, 'cause then I get a free ride home! I've done other stuff too— I've made one o' them, um, ab-isolators, you know? outta a wire hanger and two tin cans. I been ingenious 'bout this shit! I should be one of those girls on TV. I should be one o' them Spice Girls! I mean—fuck those British bitches! We need some American Spice! I could be...Southern Spice! Or Kentucky Fried Spice! I could do that! I should be selling stuff on TV. That's what I should be doing! I could be one o' them girls on those infomercials! Like, um...

(Runs to one side of the stage and mimes a very sexual selling technique rubbing the appliance.)

Buy this...

(Runs to the other side and repeats it in an even "hussier" manner.)

Buy THIS! But...I gotta get me a better wardrobe! I been stealin' all I can—hence my Merry-Go-Round handbag. But I can't do it no more—'cause I got myself caught last time I was at...Contempo Casuals...and they had this 89.95 leather skirt and I tried to like crush it up in my purse, just, you know, squish it down in there...

(Pause.)

...they weren't amused...the cops came and got me—the fuzz...and they just threw me up against the wall and frisked me, I felt just like Miss Alyssa Milano in a bad T movie of the week...I just wouldn't know what to do if I got caught again... Lord knows I can't play that Sharon Stone/Basic Instinct spread yer legs interrogation thing! I mean...I tried...

(Pause.)

...but it was a damn woman who was interrogatin' me. I just kept prayin' that she was a lesbian but—no luck. I mean, lesbians are like taxi cabs, whenever you don't need one they're everywhere, but when you need one—shit—they're no where to be found Now...what I need is for a good man ta buy me thangs 'n' make me famous...

(To someone in the audience.)

Go ahead—call me a gold digger, I don't care!! Hell, gold is in this season!

(She sashays to the other side of the stage and cozies up to a different audience member.)

Actually, right now I'm just a digger...

(Back to the other person.)

...but when I hit the gold I know you'll be jealous, girl! Right now I'm livin' off the tiny paychecks I get from the lottery—no I didn't win nuthin', I wish—I'm the girl who picks up the numbers and says 'em to the camera.

(Miming what she does on the show in a sexually charged, slow and sensual manner.)

Like "One...Fifteen"... See, it's a good job because it really fulfills part of my triple-threat training: supermodel—'cause I'm modeling the numbers, actress—'cause I gotta act like I care who wins if it ain't me and, singer—'cause, well, I hum tunes to maself when I get bored on the set. But I need somethin' better than that! So that's why I left. I mean Bubba means well, he makes a great tuna salad sandwich and he can play Janet Jackson songs doin' that underarm fart thing. But I need a more upwardly mobile-supportive environment. I can't settle! and I'm not gonna take care o' no kids till I'm ready! So that's why after my epiphany! I just know it's time to get outta here. So I'm goin' down to the Motel 6 and I'm gon' stay there until I can get enough money to go to Hollywood. And I'm changin' my name too...To Lerlene Famoos...see, you pronounce it Famoos but you spell it F-a-m-o-u-s so when you write it you see Lerlene FAMOUS! You know what else I did? I got me the same motivational book as Demi Moore says she had! She said it was the key to her success. I mean...I didn't read it yet, but...I put it in the corner of my trailer and the vibes it gives off make me feel stronger! I know if I focus, am really nice to people and get the right pair of shoes—I'm gonna make it. I just gotta be famous! *(Blackout.)*

(Barry White's multiorgasmic '70s soul begins to play as The Actor takes off Lerlene and puts on Jimmy's vest and tie—which for the moment is tied around his head—moaning and keening as if he's been poked, he drops his pants and falls to the front of the stage as the lights go up.)

JIMMY VS. THE VELVET HAMMER

(Lying on the floor, waking up.)

Oh my head! Oh my nipples!
(Looks down at his pants around his ankles.)
Oh God, it's happened again.
(To the audience.)
I've got a problem...don't laugh, 'cause it's not funny, it's causing me lots of mental stress.
(Pulls up his pants and fixes his tie.)
I've been...possessed! No it's not what you think, it's not like I think UFO's came down and took over my body and

I didn't summon up the devil or anything ... but I might as well have— Oh I'll start from the beginning—see I'm pretty shy, I always have been ... but ... I really have always wanted to be a ... STUD! You know, be tough, but tender, always says the right thing at the right time ... like those guys from the seventies like Shaft and Superfly ... But I never could be. I mean I get with a girl and my tongue would just stop—and I couldn't even form sentences. I just turn into Dork King of the Universe ... "yer pretty" is usually the best I can do. That's the best of my "repitior" ... Well, it had been a

(Makes quote marks in the air.)

"little while" since I was in a

(Makes quote marks again.)

"relationship."

(Sees audience might not be buying it.)

OK! IT HAD BEEN A REALLY LONG TIME! and I was getting a bit

(Makes quote marks.)

"lonely," if you know what I mean ... it got so bad there was a time when I just got—sex on the brain. I know you're thinking "who doesn't have sex on the brain sometimes." SOMETIMES is the key word there. It was like some tribal beating in my head—"sexSEXsexSEXsexSEXsex"—a girl could say "excuse me" when passing me in the hall and I would start to have visions of her saying "do me" ... oh boy. I couldn't do work—no even my favorite—calculus! I would just end up drawing dirty pictures and ordering the Playboy channel. I was turning into even more of a social misfit than before! It had to stop! Work was suffering, my professors were asking questions, my lab partners were getting annoyed and my little dog

Woofer was starting to look nervous. So I used all my effort to just push it down—repress it—make it go to the back of my mind— I had a mantra—NO SEX YOU MUST REPRESS NO SEX YOU MUST REPRESS— I figured I would just get it off my mind, until I really met a girl who liked me and the time was right. Oh how wrong I was. The subconscious mind is a dangerous thing—tricky—because I thought my mantra worked. I was able to do work again—do my calculus, Woofer breathed a sigh of relief... But little strange things started to happen, even though they were deeply mixed into the rest of my normal life. I'd go to buy a pair of socks—sing a little tune—"Oh I buyin' a pair a socks"—and instead I'd buy a pair of super-tight leather pants, a velvet turtleneck and a wide-brim hat with a feather, or I'd find myself casually browsing for sneakers—you know, Keds...Nikes...Dockers...but instead I'd get a pair of black, thigh-high, high-heeled boots! I mean, it all seemed normal at the time, like I needed those things...but after a while I had this strange collection of stuff. Like I was preparing for something—or someone. Then one night it all came together.

(Runs over to chair at R as the lights change to one scary blue special.)

I was sleeping in bed and this voice said

(In a deep, gruff and soulful bass.)

"Git up!"

I was shocked someone was in my apartment! So I said in my meanest voice... "Who's there?"

"It's me, boy! Git up!"

and then...my butt got slapped

(Slaps butt and continues to do so faster and faster.)

—HARD—but no one was around..and then I realized

(Looks at his hand as the slapping stops.)

it was me. I was slapping my own butt! "What's going on?" I said.

"We're going to get some boy!"

There still wasn't a light on, so I yelled... "Who are you? Where are you?"

"I'm Velvet Hammer and I'm in you!"

I didn't understand. So I jumped out of bed and flipped on the light

(Lights back up to full.)

but no one was there! I was standing in front of my mirror... and instead of seeing me in my froggies-making-toast PJs, I was in these tight leather pants, velvet turtleneck and wide-brim hat with a feather, and then I said to myself... well, my lips moved and sound came out... but I didn't want to say it...

"See boy! We look good! Had to dress us up."

"What do you mean, us? I'm ME"

"Not anymore, baby. Yo' you and me... Velvet Hammer! You brought me here yo'self! You tried to push all yer sex stuff, all yer lewd, nasty, fun desire and tried to be Mr. Nice Boy. Well, all that stuff had to go somewhere... and, baby, I am from that place... I am the silky smooth superfly superfine PIMP from the deep heart of your personality."

(Grabs his crotch.)

"'Cause tonight it's time to party! You have been celibate too long and that means the Velvet Hammer been celibate too long"

"Look! I don't know what you are—you, evil pimp spirit—but I won't let you possess me!"

"Possess you? I am you, the silkysmoothsuperfly fun part. And therefore I just want us to have a little fun! Now look, you can either help out and be aware of what's goin' on and have the best night of your life or I can just

(Goes into a '70s-style kung fu fight mode.)

Hutaa Hehtaa Huh huh Velvet Hamma!"

(Back to normal.)

"Knock yo' ass out like I did when I was dressin' us! The choice is yours."

Oh...I was at this horrible turning point—let this weird evil pimp spirit take over or try to fight? Get

(Does a Jimmy remix of Velvet's kung fu.)

HooTA Hoo-Ha...Ve-Vet Hammerrrr...knocked out?...or have the best night of my life? He was gonna do it anyway, so I said..."OK"

"Good—now just relax, let it go—Velvet Hammer's in control!"

Then it went black...

(Lights flash as theme from Shaft *plays, underscoring him.)*

I had a vague notion of strutting and singing the theme from *Shaft* as the smooth sounds of the Velvet Hammer echoing through the jungle of the night...

(Sidling over to a woman in the audience.)

"Hey, baby, my name's Velvet Hammer...'cause I'm smooth like velvet...but I bang like a hammah!"

(Moves to another woman.)

"Hey, girl...I'm industrial strength—'cause I work so hard at lovin'—oohahhchaa—I feel like a machine!"

He was handing it out...drinking it back...getting phone numbers...getting phone numbers... Me!...as this Pimp Alter Ego was having the time of my life!

(Theme music fades.)
But then I realized the more fun he was having the more I felt like I was fading...then it hit me! If I didn't take back control of my body—the Velvet Hammer part of me would never give me up. I had to get back control! So I waited till things calmed down a bit and—Velvet was doing his hair in the men's room—and then I tried to jump back in. Woop!

"What are you tryin' ta do, boy?"

"Look, Velvet, I'm taking my body back and there's nothing you can do about it!"

"Don't jive me, cat! I am just about to get to the piece of resistance of the night! The part that's gonna get us everything we want and more—I just about to strut on the dance floor!"

"Velvet, I have got control and I'm not going to give it up again."

"That's what you think, boy! I'm gonna dance if it kills me!"

Then I realized Velvet had control of one half of the body and I had control of the other...

"Hit it, Mr. DJ!"

(The funky grinding song "Pony," with its rubbery bass line and explicit lyrics, plays in the background as the battle for control over the body begins. Velvet's half trying to bump and grind, Jimmy's half trying to control it. As the dance continues we hear...)

"Velvet! Velvet, stop it stop stop...oh! Don't do it, Velvet... Not the roboto, anything but that!"

I didn't even know I could do the Running Man!

(He tries but only succeeds in making the dance more funky and illicit...the dance continues as Jimmy speaks.)

There was nothing I could do... I was fighting it hard but it only ended up making me look like I was doing a funkier and funkier chicken! But... I was also starting to like it! I was the sexy star of the dance floor—everybody wanted me. They wanted everyone to ride my pony! So I just started to go with it... and Go! And GO! And GOOOOO!

(Jimmy strikes a John Travolta pose and music stops.)
And then I blacked out...

(Lights blackout and then flash back up.)
...and I woke up, well, a lot like this—pants around my ankles and with sore nipples. I have these Velvet blackouts every weekend! Five days a week I'm nice mild-mannered bow-tie wearing, Discovery Channel watching me... and two days a week I'm this weird '70s pimp—swingin' it all over town! I thought about trying to get an exorcist to get rid of him and stuff like that, but... if I do that, I'd also be getting rid of the one good side effect of all this... THE FLASHBACKS!

(Goes into trance of ecstasy and a snippet of "pony" plays.)
Oh you're a bad girl! Bad Girl! Oh don't do that...

(Loving it.)
... don't do that...

(Snaps out of the trance.)
"WOW, WE SURE HAD FUN, DIDN'T WE, VELVET?"
"We sho did."
"But I'm tired, we gotta rest up for tonight."
"Yeah! Why don't we go to get some Aunt Bertha take-out... "
"OK! Um, can I talk to you for a minute... "

(Turns away from audience.)

"Uh, tonight can you tell those girls to go li'l easier on the nipples?"

"Sho I will, come on, Jimmy, we gotta go ... "

"Oh OK. Well, I'll see you guys later."

"I'll see *you* later, baby girl. Come on, Jimmy, let's sang it. 'If you're horny, let's do it' ... "

Ride it my pony ...

(Blackout.)

("It Isn't Working" from Woman of the Year *plays, until a door slams and the light pop up as Le Grand Director enters from offstage wearing a flowing jacket and print scarf, shouting.)*

NOTES FROM LE GRAND DIRECTOR

Jesusfuckingchrist! Bugger-fuck! Bleeding Christ! Puking Jesus! WORK! WORK! WORK! That's what we need to do, people! People, these things, this show needs to be worked on! We need to PUNCH it, whip it around, slap it on the buttocks, stick a hot poker up its butt ... this show needs an enema! This show is so bad I keep looking at my hands for fucking stigmata! Waiting for people to stick me up on a cross and sacrifice me to appease the gods of the theater that we have offended! I mean, the show is six and a half hours long! As it is now we better not invite any senior citizens to the show because some of them will be dead before Act 3. So basically, DARLINGS, you must have guessed by now I have tons of NOTES! You know, kiddies, when I was acting ... when I did or do classical text I make it live and breathe and most of all I make it SEXY! My Juliet! My Lady Macbeth! My Gertrude! My Queen Lear!

My Henrietta the Fifth! Lusty Wenches! Hell! When I played the Nurse last year at the Globe she was so sensually alive she made Juliet look like Nancy Reagan! So understand, my notes are trying to get you to come—no pun intended—at it from that angle! So sit down on your tight little buns and get ready to listen! Number 1, please stop masturbating onstage! No I don't mean literally—I don't mean that we are cutting the Romeo and Juliet masturbation sequence. NO! I mean please stop the self-aggrandizing public masturbation with the text as a lubricant. If you want to masturbate—do it in the privacy of your own homes... in front of your full-length mirrors with a strobe light or something—not on my stage! Next... all right, I have some individual notes... Latrice...

(Points to an audience member, houselights come up.)

... your scene is dry, it should be hot and wet! You are playing Cleopatra! You are a sexual, lusty bitch! You are the Queen of the Nile, you rule thousands, your loins are like the desert—large and hot as fire! Now you and Antony are in mad passionate love! The audience must know that! You must show your passion—which is a passion based in... YES! SEX! Darling, you did not just sleep with him, you didn't even just have sex with him... You RODE ON TOP OF HIM WHILE HE FUCKED YOU! Like you were a jockey riding a wild stallion! We, the audience, need to feel that! So tonight I have an exercise for you... every time you start to lose that feeling I want you to point at where that feeling is coming from, and you know where that is... your vagina! And if I don't see you doing that I will stand up in the audience and say "Point to your vagina!" Point! Vagina! Point! Vagina! Point—ME YOU doing it...all right? What? Uh-huh tough tits, dear, if you don't like to too bad!

(Houselights go down. He checks notes.)

Now let's see...also, Alise...

(Points to an audience member, houselights come up.)

...you also need a little more oomph in your scene! Now what's going on? You're trying to seduce your warrior husband who has been ignoring you! He's been off to battle...fighting with all these brawny men and slave boys and whatever, and you're a bit worried, you know? You are saying—in Shakespeare's terms—"Why hasn't thou fucked me in a fortnight!" Your voice must make him cream in his trousers! And you, Bert!—you are the other half of the scene! Must be cockier for a longer and more sustained time! As it is playing now...you come in and spill your load too soon, if you get my meaning. You're all blustery and forceful for two minutes and then you're dead in like...

(Makes sound of a heart monitor failing.)

makes me want to take electrodes and slam them on your chest and go CLEAR! "kEEE!" COME BACK TO LIFE!! Ya know? Anyway, back to the scene—you must tease her, be mean, stretch it out. Plus think where are you coming from? Where are you going? Basic stuff! I mean, you are about to get in this enormous penis of a car—a penis limousine if you will—if she doesn't catch your fancy you'll just go and do it with a thousand other bimbos! SO let's see more of that.

(Houselights go down.)

Let's see...what other small things... Simone!

(Points to an audience member, houselights come up.)

Why are you always in the bathroom? Whenever we are about to do your scenes, yer in the loo! If you don't stop going to the bathroom so much you'll never have a career in the theater!

(Houselights go down.)

And finally, people... LINES! These scenes have been around for about four hundred years—it's a bit silly not to know your part! Now, we have two more rehearsals until the audience will be here—and we are going to serve wine before and during the intermission—so they should be boozed up—but the rest is up to you. All right, now tomorrow we are going to concentrate on hair!

(Blackout.)

("The Bertha Butt Boogie" plays as The Actor returns to the coat stand and drops Le Director and revisits Aunt Bertha's booty-shakin' stance.)

AUNT B'S TV TRIUMPH

(Entering.)

No pictures, baby! No autographs right now, honey! Come down to the cafe... OK? Earl, honey, close the door! Don't let *Hard Copy* in, baby. Oh, *Hard Copy*'s after Aunt Bertha's ass! Wooo! Oh hey! I haven't seen y'all in a while.

(Putting on her glasses as she checks out the audience.)
You look good, look good... Weeell let me tell you... thangs have been crazy! You know when famous people say when they got famous it happened all so fast? Well, I always switched the channel and said, "uhuhuh..." But it's true! Girl!

Now I did do that public access show to try and get the Le Petite Cafe to stop its evil advertising... I did it just the way I wanted...Linette sang the theme song, Cousin KiKi was on the B-3—me doin' the Aunt Bertha dance... ooooh...hmmmmhmmmm... I had a live studio audience from the neighborhood, friends from church, the Fat-ass Cafe staff, all the kids...we had a good debate and a good ol' time too! In the end we all agreed that the Le Petite was wrong.

Well, I figured that was it, I was just waitin' for Mr. Le Petite to knock on my door and apologize... Well, he never came, but someone else did... PRODUCERS! In every shape and size, somebody obviously saw the show 'cause all these people wanted me to star in the real nationally syndicated *Aunt Bertha Show*! The Lord blessed me!

So now it's on! We do the shoe, the dance, the topics and...the message love yo'self! Now hold up, chile, I think I heard some people say "love yourself"! It's "love y-o-apostrophe-self"...now you try it again, babies. Good! Good! I'm still preachin' the same thing...beatin' Oprah in six markets hasn't changed me! I still keep my eye on things round here too...I make sure we tape in the morning, then porch time—watchin' out for my kiddies, then over to the Fat-Ass Cafe—which, honey, is just gettin' bigger, if you know what I mean.

You know, I never did get that apology from Le Petite Cafe, but with all the publicity from the show...they went outta business... Hee hee, Aunt Bertha's takin' over the world!... OOOh Ha ha ha! Sometimes I feel like Godzilla, child, just knockin' over buildings, knockin' over buildin's! Now y'all come down to the cafe, I'll cook you up some corn bread and chitlins and good spicy stuff...

(To girl in the audience.)
You too, girl! You don't have to try and be a supermodel, you look good just the way you are... Bye, bye, baby... bye, bye...

(Blackout.)

(Regal, dramatic and very serious classical music plays. The Actor returns to the coat stand and puts on the long velvet cape and takes up the royal walking stick of King Lear.)

HIS MAJESTY FINDS HAPPINESS

(Lear is deadly serious. He has a grim look on his face and dramatically begins to shake until he utters...)

Theater Two to your left!
(The drama grows with each occuring "couplet.")
Theater TWO!! down the hall and to the left... Theater TWO—down the hall to the left... enjoy the show! Left!

(Notices the audience.)
I am a king— I've lived a long time— I am a famous and once powerful ruler... KING—LEAR! Much has been written about me—plays, papers, theses and one slim little volume by that... bard of bullshit... William Shakespeare a.k.a. the bane of my existence. Oh, that man is to me what the *National Enquirer* is to Oprah Winfrey. Just LIES! LIES! LIES! He turned my life into an episode of goddamn *Dynasty*! I kept waiting for Joan Collins to show up!

OK—Yes it's true. I did have some trouble with my daughters. I wanted to retire and thought I would just divide my kingdom up between them equally. So I could just retire in peace—play some golf, rest a bit, you know, relax! But NO! The girls wouldn't take equal parts, they had to fight over it! You know— this time they were fighting over land, but it was actually the same goddamn fight they've been having since they were kids... Who's prettier? Who has bigger breasts? Who's handbag is more expensive—SAME OL' SHIT! But to hear Willy Shakespeare tell it, they ousted me from the kingdom and tried to kill each other and all sorts of gruesome untruths! I mean, he made Cordelia out to be some kind of selfless martyr who didn't want anything but love AND dies in the end! Now Cordelia is my daughter and I love her, but the day she is a selfless martyr is the day pigs fly out of my royal butt!

All of Shakespeare's melodrama...me beating my head screaming Lear Lear Lear, my old friend Glouster getting his eyes ripped out. All that Howl Howl Howl stuff... Yes I know the words were pretty and it was dramatic, but it was utter bullshit! And worse than that I HAVEN'T SEEN ANY ROYALTIES FROM IT. Will talked about my wrath, but wait until my lawyers get finished with him! The truth is, if you wanna hear it from Lear's mouth, I got sick of all the bickering and said, "HERE'S THE CRUSTY BOTCH OF A KINGDOM—TAKE IT!" and I got outta there!

So I thought I could then get my relaxation—move to Boca Raton or something, but because of all of the attention from the play, the media wouldn't leave me alone. So I figured—since I still wasn't getting royalties—cash in on the attention! So I booked myself on a personal appearance tour of America's shopping malls! "Meet King Lear." I thought maybe I could become King Lear Superstar! I thought I might even meet Whitney Houston! But there again the bard screwed me! He wrote most of his damn shows in that iambic pentameter stuff... DADUM, DE-DUM DEDUM DEDUM DEDUM. Well, people expected me to talk that way! I tried for a while but it just didn't work out. "I'm really glad to be here thanks a lot...for showing up...uh...I'm feeling kinda hot...and I will sign a picture here for you...if you will give the cashier the three bucks it costs. G'night, thanks!" I would slip up and some idiot would yell out, "Hey! That's not iambic pentameter." I just couldn't handle the pressure... So thanks to my greedy daughers I couldn't retire in peace, thanks to Shakespeare and his iambicfuckin'pentameter I couldn't become a jet-setting international celebrity! What was Lear going to do?

Well, I went through a very difficult phase where I tried to get a job in the private sector. I applied to all the top financial, law and management firms. I had seventy-five years of royal experience! Who wouldn't want to hire me? But people kept saying I was overqualified—that they didn't need a seventy-five-year-old former ruler. I was very depressed...I almost went slinking back to the castle just to see if I could maybe move into the belltower with the hunchback—fix it up—put in a satellite dish—catch up on correspondence—you know, I hadn't written to Macbeth in years, never did find out whether he got to be king and how that cute wife of his was...

But anyway! I never got to finish thinking about all that because I was looking through the newspaper one day and Yamamoto Theaters was showing...a revival of, well... *Showgirls*! I love that Elizabeth Berkeley. I figured it would cheer me up. I went into the theater and smelled the popcorn and saw all the people and I just felt good. Then on the way out I saw...a help-wanted sign— I thought—

(In true cliché Shakespeare acting mode.)

selling popcorn, tearing tickets. Lear could do that! Why not? So I went up and applied. What could I lose? Well, actually, I could have lost my last shred of dignity... but...I got the job! So, now I work here. I told them about my past experience and they said "Great, you're on the concession stand!" I'm GOOD too ... "Welcome to Yamamoto Theaters—would you like to try the super combo? No?"

(The lights fade ominously as thunder begins to roll.)

"Do you know who I am? King LEAR! I am brazen, force incarnate. You overwheening plebeian buttock! You're going to have a large soda, large popcorn with topping, a Kit Kat and some Gummies, or you will be gutted by my wrath!"

(Lights up to normal.)

I have the best sales record of anyone here. Yes! I'm teaching the other little ushers how to do it. Those kids, they idolize me! They're always asking "What's Juliet like?" and I'm like "wrong kingdom!" you know... But I'm happy here. People don't bow as much, but let me tell you—Friday night when some hot movie is out and I'm working the door—people get pretty close. Yes, the movies—a good place to end up. Plus Lear loves popcorn.

(Blackout.)

("I'm Beautiful Dammit" plays as The Actor drops Lear and puts a perfect scarf around the neck of the Make-over Guerrilla.)

THE MAKE-OVER GUERRILLA

This—is a satin pillow for the eyes—you just place it on your eyes if you're traveling or you just need a luxurious quiet moment. It has a raspberry organza scent. It's from Donna Karan Home $325. It's a luxury item. Sooo... What do yo think of the new collections? Fabulous, yes? Oh I know, so much polyester, but it's cut so well—I could die! Master Tailor! Master Tailor! I mean, if you had a spandex dishrag and it was cut right it could be a fabulous evening gown, for christ sake! Well... if you had the right figure for it. I see some people trying to wear some of this stuff and I say, No no no, you don't need everything to be *couture* to be stylish! But you know these logo hounds... I have one customer who refused to wear anything that doesn't have a gigantic designer logo on it! I try to tell him—I try and warn them all but they don't listen... they are just FOOLS! Oh, it makes me so angry! I just want to take them and say...

(Now violently upset and hyperventilating.)
you better dress better! You! You...

(Taking control.)
breathe! calm... Imagine the Armani runway. Clean, flowing, beautiful, relaxed, neat spring collection. I'm sorry. It's hard for me sometimes... you see, I was blessed with a second sight! Oh, it's more than just a good sense of style... it's like a spiritual connection that tells me what looks good... what doesn't and how to FIX IT! Now there

was a time when I wanted to just fix, fix, fix fixfixfixfix and I went over the "fashion edge" so to speak. You see, I was working in the cosmetics department as a "Scent Splasher" and one day they gave us all a workshop on ... MAKE-OVERS ...

(A heavenly light comes on as angels sing and thunder rolls.)

When I saw what some blush, foundation and a new outfit could do ... I heard the voice of GOD! And he told me to use my powers for good rather than evil. Rather than help beautiful people become unobtainable gods and goddesses ... I wanted to help ugly, uh ... people who need guidance ... become beautiful. I was going to become the Mother Teresa of Style! I wanted to help ... the mall people.

(Takes on the tone of a Sally Struthers Save the Children infomercial.)

You know the people I mean ... the woman in the silver muumuu and the silver lipgloss ... the unibrow man who refuses ... he refuses to pluck! You know the people I mean ... So I decided on my lunch breaks to brave the mall! I felt like I was going on the crusades with Elsa Klench! I set up a huge table with a sign that said "Style Saves" and waited to greet the masses ready to be redeemed! "Oh hello ... no white socks with dress shoes ... " "Hi! Smaller glasses or contacts, have you ever thought about that? You should ... and shorter skirt." "Stop! No muumuus ... long sweater ... cinch it! Black leggings ... little black boots ... very chic!" A few people stopped at first but then people began ... avoiding me ... and the people who did stop just ... laughed in my face! I was eventually reduced to yelling things across the mall like "EYELINER!" "Ski-lift tickets are not accessories!'' Finally I was forcibly removed from the mall by Ed the security guard for the so-called harassment of the woman in the smiley-face T-shirt and the flip-flops who just wouldn't take the hint! Well, this sent me into a downward spiral. God had sent me on a mission and I had failed! I took a sick leave from work. I just sat around the house in my Givenchy *haute couture* bathrobe watching talk shows...Ricki, Sally Jessy, Aunt Bertha...but that didn't help! It just bombarded me with more bad style choices... Hot pink spandex! Blue eye shadow! It was awful... But then, one of the shows was on MAKE-OVERS...

(Heavenly light shines as angels sing and thunder rolls.)

You see, on this show they had a stylist go with a camera crew to a random person's home and make them over! Genius! That's what I had to do! Oh, but random people weren't going to let me into their house...

(Jokingly.)

I'd probably have to break in and kidnap them or something... Heehee heee kidnap... hee he he haha ha he hmmmmmm. That was it! I had to KIDNAP people for their own good and make them over! I had to become a Make-over Guerrilla, not the animal, but the illegal freedom fighters—

(Tying the scarf from around the neck around his head Rambo style.)

—fighting to free the beauty inside you! Yes. That's where I lost it. When the idea of kidnapping and make-overs merged...I officially went over the fashion edge. Here's the edge—here's me here's the edge—here's me do-doo-doo-hello! There I went! But was determined! I began to plan my first liberation. I went back to work and began stealing—I mean storing—just a little bit at a time. When I had enough stored—plus a little for me—I had to find my lucky victim. There were so many to choose from, but after much consideration I decided on this poor trailer park girl. I saw her at the store all the time...always trying to look chic and just failing badly... I could see she had beauty deep, deep, deep, deep...inside her but she needed my help to bring it out. I actually spoke to her once when I caught her trying to steal some Donna Karan sunglasses. I didn't turn her in because I felt sorry for her. She was so grateful she just went on and on in her cute little accent how appreciative she was and how when she was a rich and famous supermodel slash actress slash singer that she'd shower me with gifts, etc. etc. So I could see she had a good heart—but she needed a good dose of fashion tough love and, thanks to my mission, she was going to get it! I had everything ready—and the next time I saw her I faked a fit of the vapors and punched out to follow Miss Thing. She was taking the bus, so I had time to get my car and my preparations and follow... After one stop at Aunt Bertha's for take-out she ended up at the Motel 6—where she was registered under Lerlene Famous...anyway, I staked out the room for the next few hours, feeling a lot like Angie Dickinson on a mission from God, and when night fell I got to work...

(*Strikes a crucifixion pose. Blackout.*)

(*"Material Girl" plays as The Actor returns to the coat stand and puts on a beautiful, expensive dress and flowing Armani-type scarf and slips offstage. The lights come up as we hear Zarzuffa's voice.*)

LERLENE HITS GOLD

(The stage is bare, we hear a familiar foreign accented voice call out.)

Darling, we have to hurry! We must get to the fancy dress ball before Claudia Schiffer so you can make a big entrance...

(Lerlene is backing into the room:)

OK, darlin', I'm just gonna be a minute, I'm still puttin' on my make-up... Oh! Y'all scared me... My bedroom's so big now I never know when people are in it... Hi! How do I look? Different, right? Thangs have been changin', changin', changin'... Do you like my outfit? It costs more than your trailer! Chanel, Escada, Armani, Valentino and Givenchy—retail price—a whole hell of a lot! I made it, girl! OOOOH, look at you...yer turnin' so red...looks like you're goin' inta the jealousy shakes! Better take a pill or somethin'. Bet y'all are wonderin' how I got so far so fast... TALENT! BEAUTY! AMBITION! Actually, it all began when I was lookin' through the newspaper for bus fares to Hollywood. I saw this big-ass two-page ad for 1-900-Zarzuffa I want to be your queen... I read it, a rich foreign man lookin' for a wife? It was a miracle! A miracle with my name tattooed all over it! So I scraped together the 2.99 to make the call and with the 1-900-Zarzuffa operator—who was really nice but I had trouble understandin' her accent—I made an appointment to meet Zarzuffa the next day! She told me I had to look my very best because Zarzuffa was very picky and he was meetin' thousands of women. That night I went through my stuff—my Contempo Casuals, my Merry-go-Round, even my twenty-dollar sweater from The Gap! But nuthin' looked right—neon pink, neon green and neon yella just didn't look good together no more... I was very depressed Zarzuffa was never gonna want me now... I was just about to sit on my bed and eat five boxes of mallomars when there was a knock at my door... Then this man slash woman slash it person busted in! I couldn't tell what sex they were but it smelled good and was very well-dressed. Then he she it said "I am here on a mission from God...I'm going to change your life." I was so depressed that all I could think was "great"! My life is in shambles and now some unisex Jesus freak is gon' kill me... But then he slash she slash it said "God has sent me to make you over..." I thought, oh my God! Two miracles in a row! God was tryin' to tell me somethin'—GET RICH QUICK GIRL MARRY ZARZUFFA! I said two amens, jumped up and down and said come on you angel let's get to work! And we worked me all night long...that unisex angel had all of Neiman Marcus and Saks Fifth Avenue out in their car. We went over walkin' and talkin' and style in the 20th century, season by season and how to make it work for me...by dawn...I made that My Fair Lady chick look like Forrest Gump! I air-kissed goodbye to the angel and I went to meet Zarzuffa... Well, I walked in there decked out lookin' fine, turnin' round...

(*The Actor turns away from the audience and speaks in Zarzuffa's voice.*)

"Darling, what are you doing? Who are you talking to?"

(*Lerlene is running offstage.*)

"I'm telling these people how we met..."

(*Zarzuffa from off:*)

"How we met? Let me finish the story."

(*The Actor enters wearing Zarzuffa's Armani jacket.*)

Let me tell you! I was sitting in this restaurant—tired and very sore and then I see this vision walk towards me. She is turning this little diner into a Paris runway! working it left and right. She is perfect, tall, blonde, stylish...I talk to her...she tells me how she wants to be famous— I say ambitious! She says that she called 1-900-Zarzuffa— I say SMART! I ASK HER TO MARRY ME THEN AND THERE! I say, Lerlene, you must be my queen. So now WE ARE MARRIED! My father is happy—Lerlene calls him Big Poppa...Lerlene is happy—she will be starring in her own musical sitcom about modeling on Fox next season and I am happy for I have finally found MY QUEEN!
(Blackout.)

("Without the One You Love" by Aretha Franklin plays as The Actor turns back up to the coat stand to change into the next character...but there are no more costumes, no more Alter Egos, there is only himself.)

I CAN MAKE IT ON MY OWN

Whenever I think about you I feel halfway between Romeo and a big dork. I feel good or like Romeo when I think about how much I was in love with you. I mean, we would be talking on the phone and we'd say goodbye and I'd go to do something else and then I'd get this overwhelming feeling and I'd have to call you up again and tell you how much I was in love with you. But then I think about what you said and what you did and I feel like a big dork—because I imagine you hanging up with me and calling up some twisted two-faced girlfriend hotline...
"Press 1 if your man loves you and you don't him. Press 2

if he just made a fool of himself over you. Press 3 if you'd like to chat with other two-faced girlfriends." "Hey, girl! Listen to wha' my man jus' did!" I know you say it's different but that's hard to believe. Yes. Yes. You say it wasn't that you didn't love me but that you realized you loved me like a friend rather than a lover... Now that first of all makes me feel great after all the sex we had. What? Did you roll over one night and think, I love him like a friend! Well, that certainly boosts my ego! It just makes me feel even dumber because I did love you like that... I...do. Oh I hate this! I start to get all mushy and sound like some Boyz II Men song and you know it just bounces off you! I just want to love you and you don't love me. You're beautiful, sensitive and talented and sweet and I'm just...well...wait a minute... What am I saying? And I'm just...what? Romeo the Dork? NO! You know what? I'm not gonna do this anymore. Romeo certainly wouldn't have killed himself if Juliet was "just a pal." And I'm certainly not gonna be a dork the rest of my life—loving you from afar... I'm good-looking and sensitive and

(In the voice of Velvet.)

smooth and

(Lerlene's voice.)

ambitious and

(Lear's voice.)

strong and

(Make-over Guerrilla's voice.)

stylish and

(Zarzuffa's voice.)

fabulous and...

and I'm funnier than you... OK, I use more Nutrasweet than you, but regardless...I deserve to have somebody who really loves me. Forget being the slacker Romeo wannabe in some sad Indy film. I'm gonna be King Lear in some big, glamorous, action-packed, four and a half hour uncut Hollywood extravaganza! I know what I'm worth and like my Aunt Bertha says... "shit, baby! It's a lot!" So you can just find someone new to string along and torment... And ya know I'm not bitter... I know you can't say I'm not bitter without really sounding bitter... But it's the truth! Something clicked, maybe self-loathing overload or something... But I don't need you anymore. See ya, Juliet... this time parting is just plain sweet. I can make it on my own.

(*Blackout.*)

END

JULIA

Virginia Coates
Villanova University

CHARACTERS

FATHER ONE: Casual but well-dressed, has a clean-cut look. A green hospital gown is lying next to him.

FATHER TWO: Also casual, but the clothes are more a working man's clothes and he is not as clean-cut looking.

PLACE: A hospital waiting room.

TIME: The present.

JULIA

SETTING: *A small hospital waiting room.*

AT RISE: *FATHER ONE is sitting alone. After a few moments FATHER TWO enters, with loud footsteps, holding a small stuffed animal. FATHER TWO can go to the coffee maker or some other activity that keeps him from noticing FATHER ONE's reactions.*

FATHER TWO. Oh man. I had to get away. Thank God a quiet place. *(No response from FATHER ONE.)* Has yours already arrived? Looks like it, since you took off the gown. They sure as hell won't let you in that room without it. Makes you wonder what they think you could give them. I mean, how do they think the kid got here. That wasn't too sterile. Right? *(No response.)* Hey, you OK? You're not going to get sick or faint, are you?

FATHER ONE. No. I'm fine. It just got a little intense in there.

FATHER TWO. Ya, I know what you mean. All that rushing around. And the yelling, by my wife, that is. She swore she was going to be calm through the whole thing. "I can handle it." She wasn't going to take any drugs. After that first contraction, they couldn't give it to her fast enough. They just gave her Demerol. That's why I could leave. I wish I could drug her up like that all the time. Wish there was time to run down for a cigarette. Told her I was just gonna run out to give an update to the family. *(Pause.)* I feel really bad for the wives though, you know? I thought mine was going to squeeze my hand off. Had to get away from it all, you know? The wife screaming, having to go give updates every fifteen minutes. I think my entire family and neighborhood is out in the waiting room. *(Pause.)* God, all those tubes in her, running every which way. It's weird to see her like that. You know what I mean? *(Pause.)* I guess you can tell this is our first, right? I've never been so nervous about nothin' in my life. How about you, this your first?

FATHER ONE. Yes, this was our first.

FATHER TWO. You got your family with you tonight?

FATHER ONE. No. Just us.

FATHER TWO. That's the way to go. That's what I told my wife. Maybe call our parents, that's it. But no, we have the entire family here, even cousins, some of our neighbors too. It's a zoo. *(Pause. Fiddles with the stuffed animal.)* Bet you're wondering what I have this for. I bought it a couple of months ago from one of the vendors down at central station. I wanted to be the first one to give her a present. Oh we're having a little girl. Found out through those ultra sounds. Did you know what you were going to have?

FATHER ONE. Yes, we knew. A little girl.

FATHER TWO. Wow, you too. Congratulations. I was thrilled when I heard it was a girl. My family thought I'd be disappointed, thinking I'd want a son first. But man, a little girl, can't wait till she starts asking me for new dresses and ballet lessons. And if my wife has her way, it'll be right away. Right. We've got the room all done up in pink. Pink wallpaper, pink curtains. Too much, I know, but what the heck. *(Pause.)* Anyway, it's stupid, I know, givin' a present, but I don't know, you want to give them so much, that's what I realized when I saw this. I want to give her everything. I won't be able to, of course, and some things she'll have to get on her own but at least I can be the first, right? *(Pause.)* I really should be getting back in there but you just need a break, know what I mean?

FATHER ONE. Yes, I know what you mean.

FATHER TWO. Hey, you sure you're OK?

FATHER ONE. Yes, I'm fine.

FATHER TWO. Well, I gotta get back in there. It's not long now, or at least that's what the doctor keeps telling my wife. I think he keeps telling her that so she won't kill him. Sure everything is all night? *(Starts to leave.)*

FATHER ONE. The baby was born dead.

FATHER TWO. What?

FATHER ONE. Our baby. She was born dead.

FATHER TWO. Oh God, I'm sorry. How could I have been so stupid, me and my big mouth. I didn't think, well, you wouldn't, you know, I'm really sorry.

FATHER ONE. We knew. We knew before we came in. She wasn't due for another two months. My wife couldn't feel the baby yesterday. She went to the doctor and there was no heartbeat. She called me at the office, told me to meet her at the hospital. I knew as soon as I heard her voice. We'd been trying for months and just like that it was over. The months of trying, all the frustration and pain to get her, all for nothing.

FATHER TWO. I'm really sorry, but you can try again, right? You'll have another.

FATHER ONE. Try again? I couldn't go through this again. It's not just the disappointment. It's the pills and the needles and the overwhelming hope, please this time, please just let this time work. *(Pause.)* I'm such a coward, I'm such a coward. My wife just had her and I couldn't stay in the room, I just had to leave.

FATHER TWO. You left her in there, with your baby. You gotta go back in there.

FATHER ONE. What the hell do you know. Your going to have a perfect baby. You probably weren't even trying.

FATHER TWO. Hey, I know enough to be a man and stand by wife and my baby even if it is dead. That's your family in there!

FATHER ONE. I don't need some plumber telling me about my family. You weren't there, you have no idea what it's like. You're going to go into your wife's room, she's going to push out your perfect baby and you're going to the waiting room with your entire family in there and you're going to celebrate with the balloons and champagne. You don't know what it's like for me. You come in here talking about your family and that damned stuffed animal. Think about what it would be like knowing your baby's going to the morgue next for an autopsy, then you can lecture me about being a man.

FATHER TWO. Hey I'm sorry, your right, I don't know much of anything and I don't know what it's like for you. But your family needs you, I do know that much.

FATHER ONE. The room was so quiet. There had been so much noise just before she was born. Telling my wife to push and me coaching her, the staff talking to each other, the monitor, all the clinks and clanks, just like I'd imagined it would be, but as soon as she came out it was silent. The baby was so dark and still, didn't make a sound. I know it's crazy but I still expected her to. She looked perfect. My wife didn't say anything but I looked at her and tears were streaming down her face. It took me a second to realize they were running down my face too. Nobody said a word, just the sound of the clinks and clanks. They cleaned her off and wrapped her in a blanket. The nurse asked my wife if she wanted to hold her. *(Pause.)*

FATHER TWO. Did she? Did she hold her?

FATHER ONE. Yes. That's when I left. I just couldn't stay there anymore and watch her hold the baby. That still bundle. It was supposed to be the happiest time of our lives.

FATHER TWO. You have to go back in there. She needs you, they both do.

FATHER ONE. Before she gave birth I thought I could do it, I had been calm through everything they threw at us. But when the nurse asked what the baby's name was, that's when I knew I couldn't take any more. I'd completely forgotten about giving her a name. That's when it became real. We lost our child.

FATHER TWO. What did you name her.

FATHER ONE. Julia.

FATHER TWO. That's a real pretty name.

FATHER ONE. We had picked it out months ago. Back when we didn't know what the sex was, we were still picking out names for both. We couldn't decide on a boy's name but a girl's we were both sure. Julia. *(Pause.)* Your wife didn't have your baby yet, right?

FATHER TWO. No, not yet.

FATHER ONE. Did you decide on a name yet?

FATHER TWO. Ya. We're going to call her Anna, after my wife's mother.

FATHER ONE. When she arrives you hold on to her tight, hold them both. *(Pause.)* I can't go back in.

FATHER TWO. Here, why don't you take this. *(Holds out the stuffed animal, FATHER ONE doesn't even look at it.)* You take this for your little girl. It'll be a present, from my Anna to your Julia. You can... You can... Julia can take it with her. *(Holds out the animal, FATHER ONE doesn't move.)* I'm gonna just leave it here. *(Sets it down next to FATHER ONE and exits. FATHER ONE sits for a moment, then picks up the stuffed animal, looks at it and sets it back down. He then stands up, puts on the hospital gown and exits. Blackout.)*

END

GOOD BUSINESS

Tom Gannon
Miami University

CHARACTERS

FRANK CAPOBIANCO: Late 20s.

JOHN FITZPATRICK: Mid-20.

PLACE: Detroit, Michigan.

TIME: The present.

GOOD BUSINESS

SCENE ONE

SETTING: *Tini's, a small, dingy bar in Detroit's east side, owned by John's brother.*

AT RISE: *It's 2:45 a.m., early summer. JOHN is behind the bar cleaning glasses when FRANK walks in.*

JOHN. Capo.

FRANK. Fitz. *(Walks behind the bar and pours a Scotch while JOHN continues to wash glasses.)* Hey, sorry. I know I said 2:30, but they were having drag races on Chalmers *(Goes to the other side of the bar and sits.)* so I watched for a little while, and then had to go down Mack and come back up some back streets.

JOHN. In Guillermo? Man, you can't be driving that car around here this time of night—

FRANK. No, not Guillermo.

JOHN. Well, what? How the hell'd you get here then?

FRANK. OK, OK, I'll answer all your questions in a minute and tell you everything about tonight. Guillermo's not with us tonight, ah, someone else is taking his place, he had other business, it's— I'll explain it all. But first, I gotta tell you this joke.

JOHN. What? *(Stops cleaning and pours a Tanqueray and tonic.)*

FRANK. This joke, this joke I heard. It's good, it's funny, and, it's also got a little lesson in it.

JOHN. Tell me the joke later, explain tonight first. I want to know about tonight.

FRANK. All in due time, my friend. All in due time. Joke first, explanation second, plan for tonight to follow shortly.

JOHN. Come on, who the fuck are you, Chris Rock? Just tell me—

FRANK. Nope. Joke first.

JOHN *(seeing that FRANK will not relent)*. Fine. Gimme the joke.

FRANK. It's funny, it's funny. You'll like it. All right? All right. OK, so there's these two guys stranded on an island after a shipwreck. One single guy and one guy with his wife.

JOHN. The wife's there too?

FRANK. Yeah, the wife too. So they're there for a while, you know, a few months, and the single guy is getting really horny. He wants to get a piece of the other guy's wife and she's kind of flirty, she seems like she'd do it, but the husband is always breathing down her neck. So this one day the single guy is sitting in the top of a palm tree. He's up there, taking his turn looking out at the ocean, looking for passing ships to rescue them, but he's thinking about how he's gonna fuck the woman. Then he gets this idea, he looks down at the couple on the beach and yells, "Hey you two! Stop that fucking!" And the two of them just look at each other wondering what the hell he's talking about because they're sitting ten feet apart. *(Pause.)* So the husband goes up in the tree the next day to take his turn as lookout. He's looking out at the ocean, doesn't see any ships, then he looks down at the beach, at his wife and the guy who

HAD been sitting apart when he climbed up, and he says, "I'll be damned. From up here it really does look like they're fucking."

JOHN. That's pretty good, man.

FRANK. But I didn't tell you that to make you laugh. I was hoping you'd find it funny, but that was a side benefit. Kind of like TV. It's only a coincidence that we are entertained by television. Television exists solely for advertisements, for companies to push cute slogans and catchy jingles—

JOHN. So what'd you tell me the joke for?

FRANK. Oh yeah, I'm trying to show you that from far away, if you yell loud enough, you might—you can, you can convince someone that things are one way even though they're not.

JOHN. OK.

FRANK. And. By the time they get to where you were, or want them to believe you were, you're the fox in the hen house, you've cracked the safe, you've fucked the wife and they're sitting back thinking everything's cool. Situation normal.

JOHN. Hey you two stop that fucking.

FRANK. Stop that fucking.

JOHN (lights a Kool). OK, the joke's been told. So. What the hell are we doing here, and what time is your man going to show?

FRANK. All in due time, my friend. All in due time. He'll be here, don't worry about that.

JOHN. So how'd YOU get here?

FRANK. Me?

JOHN. Yeah, you said Guillermo's not with us—hey, I gotta ask you, you ever get funny looks or people ask questions because you insist on everyone calling your car Guillermo?

FRANK. Sometimes. Yeah, yeah sometimes. Sometimes people ask where the name came from and I'm all in disbelief. I'll say, "Guillermo. Guillermo. Fucking Willie Hernandez." Then some people get it. But other times, I'll still get a blank stare and I'll have to say something like, "Willie Hernandez. Guillermo Hernandez. Pitcher for the Tigers? Last time they won the World Series? Fucking 1984?"

JOHN. Some people can't even really remember that.

FRANK. Great days. Great days. When Sparky still had some spark and no one would have even thought of tearing down Tiger Stadium. *(Pause, lights a Vantage.)* Yeah, so I named my car Guillermo as a tribute to Detroit. Everything that's good about this city—

JOHN. '67 Red Stang convertible—

FRANK. With the 289 under the hood and the name of a pitcher who helped bring a championship back to Motown. *(Pause, drinks.)* The fuckin' Roar of '84.

JOHN. Yeah. *(Pause.)* So what's the deal, why isn't Guillermo here?

FRANK. Scotty's got him right now.

JOHN. Scotty's the guy who's setting this whole thing up.

FRANK. Right. Scotty Sarasino. He's the one I've been telling you about. I'm telling you, this guy knows his shit, if he's setting it up, it's a lock.

JOHN. So who is he?

FRANK. He's a cool guy, you'll like him. And hey, he's got a General Lee.

JOHN. A what?

FRANK. A General Lee, you know, like—

JOHN. Like Bo and Luke Duke?

FRANK. Yeah—

JOHN. So is it a real '69 Charger or one of those bullshit kit deals?

FRANK. '69 Dodge Charger complete with a 440 big block magnum V8, the doors welded shut and the numbers zero-one on each side.

JOHN. So this guy drives around in an orange car with a Confederate flag on the top of it.

FRANK. Yes.

JOHN. The fuckin' rebel stars and bars on the roof of his car.

FRANK. Yes.

JOHN. But this is Detroit, we're Yankees. We are not Southern in any way. And let's be honest with ourselves, Confederate flags just ain't the smartest things to have in Detroit. Especially on top of your car.

FRANK. Give the guy a break. You don't even know him. He just loves the *Dukes of Hazzard*. In fact, well, I... nah, I shouldn't.

JOHN. What?

FRANK. Well, the show kind of fucked him up if you ask me.

JOHN. How?

FRANK. He had a thing for Daisy when he was younger.

JOHN. So? I had a thing for Daisy. Everyone had a thing for Daisy, didn't you?

FRANK. Well, yeah, but... but he really had a thing for her.

JOHN. What do you mean?

FRANK. Well, ah, who's the actress that played Daisy?

JOHN. Catherine Bach.

FRANK. Ah dammit! Dammit! Yes. Yes. Catherine Bach. Catherine Bach. Hm. Yeah. Anyway, when he was eighteen, he's like thirty-five now, so when he was eighteen the show was right at its peak.

JOHN. Yeah.

FRANK. Well Scotty was so infatuated with Daisy—Catherine Bach, that he moved out to L.A. because he was in love with her and he was convinced that they were soul mates.

JOHN. So what happened?

FRANK. Well he got caught trying to sneak onto the set at Warner Brothers and when they searched him, they found love letters that he'd written to her. They gave him a choice, get his ass back to Motown or simmer awhile in an L.A. prison.

JOHN. That can't be constitutional.

FRANK. Constitutional or not, they made the same threat to many lovesick men who had come to L.A. with the same thing in mind.

JOHN. Other guys went out there thinking Daisy Duke was their soul mate?

FRANK. Yeah. That shit happens to almost every celebrity. People get obsessed. It's strange what people will do because of fame.

JOHN. Or money.

FRANK *(pause)*. Or money.

JOHN. Speaking of money... *(Pours another Tanqueray and tonic and another Scotch for FRANK.)*

FRANK. Yeah?

JOHN. What's the job?

FRANK. Oh it's fuckin' beautiful. He's got this thing for us that he's checking on right now. There's this Jewish furrier in West Bloomfield—

JOHN. Ho. Wait a minute. We got to go way the fuck out to West Bloomfield? You never said West Bloomfield—

FRANK. Keep it in your pants, my man, lemme finish—

JOHN. No, but see, West Bloomfield, that's way the fuck out there, man. And we're robbin' a Jew? Christ. Jesus fuckin' Christ. Do you know what they'll do to us if we get caught? Huh? We're talking a huge difference between pulling a job here, where the cops got bigger fish to fry, and out there where they'd nail our asses to the wall because we crossed the Eight Mile border. Those suburb faggots take down anything from Detroit as hard as they can, black or white—and don't think we'd get off easier because we're white. Fuck no. They'd probably come down on us twice as hard. They want us to stay on our side and they'll stay on theirs and it'll all be all right, but once anyone from HERE tries to do some business out THERE it's fuckin' showtime. Fuckin' Showtime at the Apollo. They think they gotta make an example of us. No man, I don't like it. I think we should stay on this side of Eight Mile. (Pause.) It's just good business.

FRANK (pause). Are you done? Are you finished spewing your paranoia? You are? Good. Now listen, listen to me. If HE checks it out and says it's OK, then it's OK.

JOHN. Yeah, but a furrier? I mean, I don't know anything about that and you don't either—I know you don't. Neither of us would know a mink from a chinchilla from a fox from a fucking possum. And how're we gonna unload it? And security? Furriers definitely got security. I don't know shit about 'em, but I know they got tight security. *(Brief pause.)* Especially Jewish ones.

FRANK. Look, look, like I said, if he checks it out, it's OK. He's got a man on the inside and he's got people to move it—

JOHN. If he's got people to move it, why can't he find anyone to do the job? Why's he picked us? We've never done big jobs, Capo. We're smalltime guys—

FRANK. Yeah, but we're good. We're fuckin' good. We both got sort of regular jobs, you work in your brother's bar and I work for my dad's company—

JOHN. You draw a check from your father's company.

FRANK. Hey. Hey. I work there. I do work.

JOHN. When you feel like it. When you're not too hungover, which is like two days a we—

FRANK. Fuck you. OK? Fuck you running. You're— *(Pause.)* You're missing the point. What I'm saying to you is this. We are good thieves. We proved ourselves to Scotty—

JOHN. How?

FRANK. He was aware of the job we pulled in March. He—

JOHN. March? March? Aw Jesus! Capo, we robbed a little tiny bakery in Hamtramck! Some eighty-five-year-old Polack lady behind the counter! What'd we take, sixty-three dollars and some fuckin' cupcakes? Jesus, Frankie—

FRANK. Hey. Hey. It's not the amount. At all. It's not the amount we took that matters. What matters is that we went in there like professionals—

JOHN. Professionals? We wore nylons on our heads and that made us professionals?

FRANK. Hey. Are we still here? Free, I mean. Are we locked up? Cops come looking for us, huh? Did they?

JOHN *(muttering)*. Felt bad too, taking money from an old woman like that—

FRANK. The point IS, we did a job. LIKE PROFESSIONALS. And we have steady jobs. Real jobs. Legit jobs. That takes heat off us and off Scotty. *(Pause.)* And he knows me. He knows I'm reliable, that I can be trusted. Huh? See? And since you're the only one I've ever worked with, I vouch for you, he's OK with you. Everybody trusts each other, everybody wins. *(Pause.)* And we need this. I need this, you need this. Huh? You need this. Nicki's been pressuring you to have a kid, right? Get a better job, start thinking about moving to the suburbs—

JOHN. Fuck the suburbs, I wanna live my entire life in Corktown.

FRANK. Yeah, but does Nicki? And does she want your kids growing up there? Do you want your kids growing up there? And what about when Tiger Stadium's gone? Does Corktown still have the same appeal? The Cavanaugh days are gone, my friend. This is no place for a family.

JOHN. How'd we make it through?

FRANK *(pause)*. We were lucky. *(Pause.)* Think about all our friends who didn't make it, killed, drugs, jail—

JOHN. That's what I'm saying! Jail!

FRANK. Freshen up the drinks, please. *(JOHN does so.).* We are not going to get caught. *(He lights a Vantage.)* I promise you, we will not get caught. This is a chance,

Fitzy. A real chance to make a real score. Thousands of dollars in untraceable cash—

JOHN. And what about the IRS, Frank? Huh? I don't know anything about hiding money, I mean what if they do a thing, you know? What if they, uh, audit me? What if I get audited and they find thousands—

FRANK. That's not a problem in the least. OK, I can show you how to do that, but right now, I need you to calm down and get ready to do a job. *(Pause.)* Are you calm now? All settled? *(JOHN lights a Kool.)* Good. *(He scans the bottles behind the bar.)* You got Crown Royal, you got any RC?

JOHN. RC?

FRANK. Yeah, Royal Crown cola.

JOHN. No, but I got some Coke.

FRANK. Coke's no good. We need some RC. He'll be pissed if there's no RC.

JOHN. He won't drink Coke?

FRANK. No, his drink is Crown Royal and RC. Crown Royal and Royal Crown. No Jack and Cokes, no Beam and Cokes, hell, no Crown Royal and Coke. Only Crown Royal and RC.

JOHN. Well what happens if we don't have any RC?

FRANK. Lemme tell you a story. We were in a bar—

JOHN. Where?

FRANK. Somewhere in Southfield, I don't remember. Anyway we were in this bar and he ordered a Crown Royal and RC. And the bartender laughed and said "RC? You want a fuckin' moon pie with that?" Scotty went nuts, jumped over the bar after this fuckin' guy, insulting his family, his sexual habits, the whole thing.

JOHN. Yeah.

FRANK. So there's two bottles of Crown Royal behind the bar. He throws this guy around, punching him, choking him, just all around giving him the business. He gets the guy on his knees and tells him to pray. So this guy, this dumbass college kid with an earring and goatee, this kid is shitting his pants. He puts his hands together like this *(Praying.)* and looks up all scared and says, he says to Scotty, "What should I pray for?" And Scotty says to him, "Repeat this prayer after me, Hail Mary full of grace," and the kid does it, and then he says, "I pray this bottle don't break my face." And the kid looks up, he's got that deer-in-the-headlights expression, and he's just babbling "No, no, please, don't, sir, please," and this guy who came with him, some guy I've never seen before or after this night, this bigass Chaldean, pulls out a straight razor straight outta nowhere, and he says, with a really heavy accent, he says, "Hey man, you say what he tell you to say or I carve his name on your forehead."

JOHN. What the hell were the other people in the bar doing?

FRANK. Other people in the bar were gone, man. Once they heard the things Scotty was saying, it was MEEP MEEP and feets don't fail me now.

JOHN. So what the hell happened?

FRANK. He tossed me one of the bottles and tucked the other one under his arm. So the kid says what he was told to say and Scotty, it's like he doesn't really hear the kid, but when the kid's done talking, he says, "This was a warning. Never make fun of a man's drink. Drinking is serious business. A MAN'S business. If you can't handle that with respect, get a new job."

JOHN. Jesus. *(Pause.)* And we're going to work for this guy? He sounds like a fuckin' psycho.

FRANK. Yeah, but there's a method to his madness.

JOHN. I fuckin' hope so. *(Pours fresh drinks.)* I hope he doesn't flip out because we don't have any RC. *(Pause, they clink glasses and drink.)* I also hope he gets here before I start collecting my goddamn social security.

FRANK. He'll be here, remember, he's got Guillermo.

JOHN. Yeah, what the hell's going on with that?

FRANK. What?

JOHN. You said he had a General Lee.

FRANK. He does.

JOHN. Why'd he borrow your car then?

FRANK. What?

JOHN. If he's got a General Lee, why'd he borrow Guillermo?

FRANK. Oh, I asked him the same thing. He said he needs a car that won't identify him, he wanted to go incognito. And a classic Stang in the rich burbs doesn't really stand out much, but the General Lee is pretty conspicuous around here.

JOHN. A General Lee is conspicuous in Alabama, this is fucking Motown.

FRANK. That's my point.

JOHN. Fuckin' A.

FRANK. Yeah.

JOHN *(brief pause)*. Well do you have the General Lee?

FRANK. No, that'd defeat its own purpose.

JOHN. Well what the hell'd you drive over here?

FRANK. He gave me an old Pontiac, one of those bigass Bonnevilles, it's the car we'll take on the job.

JOHN *(shaking his head).* Christ. *(Phone rings, they look at each other, JOHN answers it.)* Tini's. Oh hey babe. *(Pause.)* Yeah, Frank's here now. We're just about to boogie on outta here. *(Pause.)* Yeah. *(Pause.)* Jimmy Sawicki's. Mmm-hmm. Yeah. *(Pause.)* I'll be home at six. *(Pause.)* No. Please, c'mon, don't wait up, six o'clock in the *morning. (Pause, smiles.)* All right. I'll see ya then. Love you too. *(Hangs up.)*

FRANK. Nicki?

JOHN. Yeah.

FRANK. What's the whole thing about Jimmy Sawicki?

JOHN. I told her he was having an all-night poker party we were going to.

FRANK *(laughs).* All-night poker party?

JOHN. Yeah. What the hell else could I say? Huh? She can't know about this.

FRANK. I know.

JOHN. Yeah?

FRANK. Yeah. *(Brief pause.)* Shit. *No* one can know about this.

JOHN. Good. As long as we're clear on that.

FRANK. Well what're you gonna tell her when you come struttin' in like Daddy Warbucks?

JOHN. You and me went to Windsor and got real lucky at the craps tables.

FRANK. Craps huh? *(laughs.)* Not just a big night of hot hands at Jimmy Sawicki's all-night poker party?

JOHN. No, don't fuck around, man. Craps.

FRANK. Yeah. Yeah, that's good. That's a good cover you gave to Nicki too. Jimmy Sawicki. Huh. I had to shake down some guy who looked like Jimmy Sawicki today.

JOHN. Oh. You actually *did* work today.

FRANK. Yeah, I actually did. My dad bought up this guy's debts and they sent me out to see if I could collect anything.

JOHN. Where'd he live?

FRANK. Ah, this trailer park in Warren.

JOHN. You get any money out of him?

FRANK. No, but listen to this. I go out there, and this guy, this unemployed asbestos remover, he invites me in. I do the whole, "I'm here to collect," he gives me, "I still can't find a job." Whatever. But. This was worth the whole trip. His trailer is split into two sections. One where he hangs out during the day, watches NASCAR, drinks Colt .45, hosts dinner parties, all that shit. The other room though, where he sleeps, that room isn't really a bedroom at all—

JOHN. What is it? A dungeon for sex games?

FRANK. No. *(Pause.)* It's a shrine. A shrine dedicated to Evel Knievel.

JOHN. What?

FRANK. Yeah. This guy has two rooms and one is a shrine to Evel Knievel. Autographed pictures, posters, action figures, he's even got an autographed cast from a broken arm Knievel got in one of his crashes. All kinds of crazy shit.

JOHN. No shit?

FRANK. No shit. This guy's showing me everything and explaining how it relates to Evel's life, his most successful jumps, his worst crashes, all the bones he broke, how many total days he spent in hospitals—

JOHN. —How many times he jacked off thinking about Farrah Fawcett—

FRANK. Exactly. Just all these off-the-wall facts no one knows. He also told me that Richard, his first name, well Richard had to choose a nickname when he decided to enter the daredevil business.

JOHN. Richard is Evel Knievel's first name?

FRANK. Yeah. But he took several months to decide on "Evel," which he ultimately did after his agent pleaded with him. But this guy was telling me that he chose "Evel" over "Retrieval Knievel," "Boll Weevil Knievel," and, ready for this? "Pastie."

JOHN. "Pastie"?

FRANK. Yeah.

JOHN. You believe this guy?

FRANK. Yeah. Why not?

JOHN. I don't know. It just sounds like "Evel" would stand out right away.

FRANK. Well yeah, it seems that way.

JOHN. I don't know if I can really buy into that, I think it would've taken about two seconds to decide on "Evel" over "Pastie." I mean come the fuck on, "Pastie" sounds like a cheap drag-queen name.

FRANK. Well I believe him.

JOHN. You do.

FRANK. Yeah. He's the best authority on Evel Knievel I've ever met.

JOHN. So he says. I don't know, it just sounds like— (FRANK pulls out .38 Special and checks it.) The fuck do you have that for?

FRANK. Just in case the situation demands it.

JOHN. No.

FRANK. No, what? John.

JOHN. No guns.

FRANK. No guns?

JOHN. No guns.

FRANK. But what if we need a gun?

JOHN. We won't.

FRANK. But we might run into—

JOHN. Look. No guns. If you have a gun, someone's gonna get shot.

FRANK. Not necessarily.

JOHN. Yes. If you have a gun it *will* go off. It has to. *(Brief pause.)* It's a rule.

FRANK. What rule? Whose rule?

JOHN. I don't know. Murphy's. Murphy's Rule.

FRANK. *Murphy's* Rule?

JOHN *(uncertain)*. Yes.

FRANK. I thought it was Murphy's *Law.*

JOHN. No it's Murphy's Ru—look, just don't bring the fuckin' gun!

FRANK. All right, fine, fine.

JOHN *(pause)*. Where the fuck is he?

FRANK. Don't worry, he'll be here.

SCENE TWO

(Later. JOHN is disinterestedly throwing darts and pacing. FRANK is in the same position.)

JOHN. So where is he?

FRANK. I don't know.

JOHN. This is trouble,

FRANK. Have another drink, be cool, he'll be here.

JOHN. Man, this is asking for trouble, this is begging for trouble.

FRANK (*walks behind the bar and makes JOHN a fresh Tanqueray and tonic*). Here, sit down, pacing isn't going to get him here any faster.

JOHN. You're sure he knows it's this bar?

FRANK. Yes. He knows where to go.

JOHN. This is trouble.

FRANK. Settle down.

JOHN. This is banging on Mr. Trouble's door late at night, man. It's after four in the morning, we're kicking Mr. Trouble's door, calling his wife a whore and screaming to Mr. Trouble's neighbors that we knocked up his slut of a daughter. He's coming down the stairs two at a time and when he gets to the porch, there is going to be a reckoning. (*Pause, he feels his pocket.*) Shit. Out of Kools.

FRANK. You want a Vantage? (*Tosses pack.*)

JOHN. Yeah. (*Lights cigarette, sits down, takes a drink.*) Mr. Trouble is one pissed-off fuck. (*Pause.*) Ah fuck it, what time is it?

FRANK. Four thirty-seven.

JOHN. Four thirty-seven? Fucking 4:37?! Jesus Christ on a crutch! What time did he tell you he'd be here?

FRANK. Between three and 3:15.

JOHN. Oh, so no big deal, he's just an hour and a half late. I mean, I mean, shit! How are we gonna do this job before daylight? He's, he's just, mmmgod, FUCK!

FRANK. I just heard a car pull up.

JOHN. About fucking time! (*Opens the door, looks out, closes the door quickly, but quietly.*) Frank.

FRANK. What? He here?

JOHN. Frank.

FRANK. What? Open the fuckin' door for him.

JOHN. It's a cop.

FRANK. What?

JOHN *(hisses)*. It's a cop. There is a fucking POLICEman in my brother's parking lot.

FRANK. OK, OK. Settle down. It's prob—

JOHN. The cops are here. Here. At my brother's bar.

FRANK. Look out and see what he's doing.

JOHN *(muttering to himself)*. A fucking cop. Believe this shit?

FRANK. What's he doing?

JOHN *(looks out)*. He's on the phone.

FRANK. The pay phone outside?

JOHN. No, the one in the food court at Northland Mall. Yes, the fuckin' one outside. *(Looks out again.)* He's lightin' a cigarette. Laughin'. *(Pause.)* He hung up.

FRANK *(pause)*. He back in his car?

JOHN *(pause)*. Yeah.

FRANK *(pause)*. He leavin'?

JOHN *(pause)*. Yeah. *(Brief pause.)* He just pulled out. Jesus. *(Brief pause.)* The fucking po-lice. *(Brief pause.)* Where the hell is he? The cops show up, but he can't grace us with his fucking presence?

FRANK. Look, he'll be here any minute. Phone-call-makin' cops aside, we have to learn the details now and do the job tomorrow night, fine, that's what we'll do. I don't know why you're flipping out. Technically, we're not involved in anything yet. *(Pause.)* The cops can't touch us, we got nothing to lose.

JOHN. Nothing to lose, huh? *(Pause.)* What about Guillermo?

FRANK. What about Guillermo?

JOHN. How well do you know this guy, huh? How well do you know this fuckin' guy?

FRANK. Pretty good. You know, I mean, I've worked for him a few times—

JOHN. What did you do for him? Didja hold his dick while he pissed? What? How well do you know this guy?

FRANK *(angrily)*. Well enough.

JOHN. Well enough? The fuck is that, well enough.

FRANK. Well enough. I know he's a professional—

JOHN *(disgusted)*. A professional.

FRANK. And that means he knows how good business works—you don't fuck your partners over.

JOHN. Partners? How the hell are we his partners? He's never even met me. What can we do for him that he couldn't already do himself? *(Pause, slowly, quietly, deliberately.)* I'll tell you what. We could trade him a Shiny Red Classic Mustang Convertible for a Heap of Shit Pontiac Bonneville. Do you hear me? He conned you. He's got your fuckin' car and he's not bringing it back. Guillermo is—

FRANK *(slams his glass on the ground)*. I said, don't worry. *(Brief pause.)* He'll be here.

SCENE THREE

(Six in the morning, JOHN is quietly sweeping up and FRANK is still sitting at the bar, with his head down in his folded arms.)

JOHN. Hey uh, Frank, it's...six. *(Pause.)* Listen, man, I got to get home. My wife.

FRANK (*looks up but not at JOHN*). Yeah. Your wife'll wonder where you've been.

JOHN. It's just—I told her I'd be home by six. (*Pause.*) I thought we'd be— I mean you told me—

FRANK (*defeated*). Yeah. I told you we'd be done by six. It's fine. It's, uh, it's fine.

JOHN. Well. You can stay, you should stay, you should, and wait. Have a few drinks. Lock up when you leave. And, uh, when he, when he gets here and tells you the plan and, uh, everything, give me a call.

FRANK. Sure. Yeah. I'll call you.

JOHN. OK then. (*Starts for the door.*) I'll see you later on today.

FRANK. Yeah.

JOHN. And, uh, um, tell Scotty I can't wait to meet him, I really want to see that Gener— (*Pause.*) Just call me.

FRANK. Yeah. (*JOHN hesitates for a moment, then walks out the door. Brief pause, then FRANK gets up and goes behind the bar to pour himself another Scotch. He goes to his shift pocket for a cigarette, but realizes that he is out of Vantages. He searches his pockets for change, but finds none.*) Aw fuck. (*He discards the pack, sits, and slowly stirs the drink with his finger. Blackout.*)

END

APRIL

Alison Fields
University of North Carolina, Greensboro

CHARACTERS

EVE: Mid-20s.
BEN: Mid-20s.
BEATRICE: Late 20s.
SIMON: Mid-20s.
HENRY: Early 30s.
DAVID: Mid-20s.

PLACE:
A large east coast city, somewhere north of Virginia.

TIME:
This April.

APRIL

SCENE ONE

SETTING: *Front porch of a small house. A door leads inside. A railing with a single column is R. Centered is an old wicker sofa. Various porch accessories—plants, wind chimes, et al, may be spread around the furniture. Two steps lead down off a platform.*

AT RISE: *Sunday afternoon. BEN and EVE are sitting on the right-hand side of the steps. BEATRICE is sitting left. BEN is holding EVE's hand.*

BEN. ...so we were driving out the River Road last Sunday in Eve's car with the top down. The weather was great, music just right, wind blowing a little. It was kinda cinematic, everything well-timed and Eve was singing along with the song on the radio. The kind of afternoon when you can almost believe everything is right with the world, And in a flash everything, well, it, it...

BEATRICE. Ben?

EVE. Go on. Tell her.

BEN. It was an incredibly romantic moment. How was I supposed to notice a small, rather inconspicuous, detour sign?

EVE. Peripheral vision?

BEATRICE. Oh my God...

EVE. And then he just happened not to notice when we drove into a foot and a half of standing water, just past the "Road Closed" sign.

BEN. I was distracted...

EVE. So we spent the next half-hour wading through muddy water, trying to push the car onto dry land.

BEN. I apologized.

EVE. He groveled.

BEN. I promised her nights on the town and dozens of roses...

EVE. A nice gesture. Didn't fix anything. But a nice gesture...

BEN. And I really tried to get the car out of the puddle, but...

EVE. But we had to call a tow truck.

BEATRICE. Oh, Eve, your poor car...

EVE. Car, yes, CAR is the operative word. Contrary to what some may believe, it is not a boat. *(Nudges BEN playfully.)*

BEN. I said I was sorry.

EVE. You're a walking catastrophe... but I find that strangely attractive.

BEN *(kisses her)*. You're too kind.

BEATRICE. So that's why I haven't seen your car all week.

EVE. That'd be the reason.

BEN. I've been instructing her on the finer points of public transportation.

EVE. Learning experience, but I'm glad I don't have to take the bus again for a while.

BEN. Snob.

EVE. Slacker. *(To BEA.)* How was the garage sale?

BEATRICE. We made a couple hundred dollars on basement junk and broken appliances. I guess that's successful. I finally persuaded Henry to part with his outgrown college wardrobe. Ripped band T-shirts, torn blue jeans, old sneakers—that kinda thing. From his rebellious days.

BEN. Henry had rebellious days?

BEATRICE. I'd say so. He took up computers when he found out that though talent is not always a prerequisite for being a rock star, it's definitely helpful. You should ask Eve. I think he actually wrote songs for her.

BEN. You sure this is the same Henry I know?

BEATRICE. The one and only. He was angry and self-righteous and completely obnoxious. Fortunately for me, he saw the error of his ways. Those were the days, I guess.

EVE. They were terrible...the songs, I mean.

BEATRICE. Anyway, Ben, I brought you a present. *(Slides a stack of books from behind her.)* I guess no one wanted these. We had them in the nickel box with my old curling iron and a bunch of scarves my grandmother gave me. I thought I'd see if you wanted them. You're the only person I know who still reads.

BEN *(flipping through stack).* You sure you want to give these away?

BEATRICE. All Henry reads are computer magazines, and I've been on the same paragraph of the book you lent me for the past six months. I think these are safe to part with.

BEN. Well, thanks. They look great. *(Scoops up books and stands.)* I've gotta take off. Run a couple errands. Take videos back. I'll see you later, Bea.

BEATRICE. See ya.

BEN *(to EVE)*. I'll be back in a couple hours.

EVE *(stands)*. Take your time. I've got things to do too.

BEN *(embraces her)*. Bye.

EVE. Bye. *(BEN walks off R. EVE returns to her seat.)* Well...

BEATRICE. Glad you survived the car crisis.

EVE. Just the latest in a long line of Ben disasters. Stay tuned for the next week's calamity—messy at the time, but guaranteed to be hilarious in retrospect.

BEATRICE. You OK?

EVE. Just peachy.

BEATRICE. Eve...

EVE. It's been a stressful week with the car, and work, and Ben. You know, that was an awfully nice gesture giving him those books, considering...

BEATRICE. Considering that I don't love Ben? I'm leaving town next week, moving three thousand miles away. He's your problem, not mine. Besides, I guess maybe he's growing on me. It's not like I hate him...

EVE. You just think I'm wasting my life with him. This is a familiar refrain.

BEATRICE. You're awfully touchy today. I've never been that harsh.

EVE. He's hopelessly in love with me.

BEATRICE. I'm not blind, Evie. He's always giving you that sad-eyed look, and he's so affectionate, and loyal... Kind of like a puppy.

EVE. Bea.

BEATRICE. Sorry.

EVE. As I was saying— He's been talking long-range plans.

BEATRICE. The "m" word? Didn't you tell me you were allergic to commitment?

EVE. That was years ago. Anyway, he's never actually said it. We've just talked around it. You know, passing conversations, feeling out each other's ideas. At least until last Sunday before the car broke down on the river road when he looks over and says...

BEATRICE. You didn't.

EVE. Yes. I told him yes, I would love to go downtown and get some Chinese later. *(Laughs.)* He didn't ask, hasn't asked. I was just testing your reaction. I guess you were paying attention.

BEATRICE. It wasn't funny. I get worried you know, that he might ask you and you might...

EVE. What? Say "I do"? Anything's possible.

BEATRICE. Are you in love with him?

EVE. He says things no one has ever said to me, holds my hand in a certain way, almost like a little kid. Doesn't expect anything of me. I've never been with anyone quite like him.

BEATRICE. You didn't answer my question.

EVE. Do you love Henry?

BEATRICE. Of course.

EVE. Honestly?

BEATRICE. Usually, OK. I usually love Henry.

EVE. OK then. I usually love Ben. I don't tell him that. He's a romantic, likes love as an absolute.

BEATRICE. He's a mess, Eve.

EVE. He's a good mess.

BEATRICE. He has no future. He answers telephones, for crying out loud. I doubt even Ben could speak poetically of his job.

EVE. He doesn't have any pretensions. Says it gives him plenty of time to think.

BEATRICE. You could do better. Hell, you have done better.

EVE. I'm sick of playing second fiddle to career ambitions. With Ben, his priority is me.

BEATRICE. That's awfully selfish, hon.

EVE. It's honest. Besides, I've never been one to gauge successful relationships by the size of a checking account. At least I'm not dating a streetsweeper, or a dishwasher, or...

BEATRICE. Henry used to wash dishes.

EVE. My point. In his "angry, obnoxious" stage, right?

BEATRICE. You have a good memory. But he's not doing it anymore.

EVE. So what? Doesn't matter to me. Dishwashing, telemarketing, whatever. It's just a way to pay the bills.

BEATRICE. I don't think I'll tell Henry you said that. You've changed a lot, you know?

EVE. That's beside the point.

BEATRICE. I haven't caught you slumming it for years— at least, romantically speaking.

EVE. Bea—

BEATRICE. I just tell it like it is.

EVE. If this is some ploy to get me...

BEATRICE. I just think if I find the right argument one of these days I might get it through your stubborn...

EVE. And I told you last time how I felt. It's useless, Bea, you might as well quit while you're ahead. Get used to it.

BEATRICE. I hate seeing you do this to yourself.

EVE. You're moving to the West Coast in three days. Unless your vision is really superb, I don't think you'll have to anymore. Besides, it's almost summer. Strange things always happen to me in the summer.

BEATRICE. This time last year, we were having a very similar conversation about David.

EVE. Whom, if I recall, you largely approved of...

BEATRICE. I have good instincts about people. Of course now we'll never know. You had that night in the city.

EVE. Changed everything.

BEATRICE. I'll say. You haven't been the same since.

EVE. It was significant.

BEATRICE. I've never heard of a one-night stand having such a profound effect. Was the sex really that good, my strange friend?

EVE. It wasn't the sex...although that was nothing to complain about...

BEATRICE. You're really vague.

EVE. I know I've told you this before.

BEATRICE. You've always been really vague.

EVE. Maybe I should tell you now. Since you're leaving...

BEATRICE. A few concrete details would be nice.

EVE. You probably won't understand. Nobody understands.

BEATRICE. Give me a little credit. I've known you since you were thirteen.

EVE. And I know I've told you this before.

BEATRICE. Not to my recollection.

EVE *(walks away from the step)*. It was June. And David took me to this restaurant by the park downtown. The one he liked so much, with the candles and the red walls. I met him at eight o'clock and we sat at a table by the window. I wore the blue dress. The one you helped me pick out. David always complimented me when I wore it.

(Lights up L. DAVID walks into light.)

DAVID. You look beautiful... I've always loved that dress.

DAVID.	EVE.
Tonight is special.	And he tells me tonight is special.

EVE *(walks to DAVID)*. and I try to ignore the way his eyes look so different. The way I feel uncomfortable. How everything he does is over-nice and not quite real.

DAVID. Waiter. Your best champagne.

EVE. We chat about this and that. I don't think anything important is said. Just that I keep staring at him. Noticing little details. How his face is not in proportion and how his tie is slightly askew. That there is a tiny tomato-sauce stain on his cuff. I listen to his voice, the way his words always sound just right.

DAVID. I've been investing in this black sheep of a software company out of California...

EVE. And how he never seems to worry about what he says.

DAVID. Of course it's risky with the market being what it is. Collins thinks I'm a fool for doing it...

EVE. How he is overconfident.

DAVID. But I know what I'm doing. I'm certainly not going to lose my shirt. I'm anticipating an upward trend...

EVE. And I realize I am trying to listen, when it should come naturally.

DAVID. Do you understand what I'm staying, honey? I'm going to make a lot of money for us...

EVE. I'm working to keep my face in the same expression, pleasant and interested. And I can hear all the other voices mumbling behind his and the static over the music. And I have to concentrate to keep from drawing back when he touches my hand.

DAVID. Eve, there is something I have to say.

EVE. And I feel it coming. My dress feels too tight and the room rocks a little.

DAVID. I've loved you for a long time. Respected you. You mean so much to me.

EVE. And I see him pulling something from his pocket. In his fist. He smiles tight like he always did, and I hear the creak of the box.

DAVID. I feel that now is the most advantageous time for us to consider investing in our joint future. That being said...

EVE. And I can't breathe and I feel trapped and everything feels fake.

DAVID. Will you marry me?

EVE. I jump out of my chair and nearly run out of the restaurant, shoving away the customers at the door, just 'cause I need to breathe, and I didn't mean for things to get so damn serious.

BEATRICE. And then you met this other guy?

EVE. He helped me out. *(Walks R, past porch.)* I don't remember walking until I look up and realize I don't know where I am. And I guess it starts raining about that time. Summer shower, a regular downpour, and here I am in the middle of a neighborhood I've never been to in the dark, all alone. *(Walks back LC.)* So I find one of those covered bus stops and sit down to think about all that has happened. It occurs to me, only then, how crazy I'm acting, and I start to feel a little scared about where I am, and out of nowhere this guy walks up to me.

(SIMON walks on, L.)

SIMON. You all right?

EVE. I don't know why. I just start talking, telling him everything about myself, about that night, and we sit together on that bench in the rain for hours, until the last bus stops for the night. He laughs and tells stories, and we smoke damp cigarettes from his pocket. I find myself falling for him almost automatically. When he invites me back to his apartment, I don't feel uncomfortable. It seems like the most natural thing in the world. He is safe and unsafe at the same time. And so different from David, and all the men at work.

BEATRICE. You just went home with him?

EVE *(walks C)*. Yeah. There was so much I didn't think about. Just start following him home in the rain. He lives in this old building in that neighborhood, up three flights of stairs. This big white room, mostly empty, except a couple chairs and a sofa and a bed in one corner. He tells me he hasn't been in town for very long.

We drink a bottle of cheap wine and talk until dawn and when the light shines through his windows we walk up to the rooftop and watch the sun reflect in the mirror buildings and I think I can see everything, past the city and to the bay. And we come back downstairs and make love. Sleep all day. Wake in the afternoon and make love again.

(Lights fade on porch. EVE crawls into bed with SIMON.)

EVE. It was only after the second time that I finally asked his name. He said it was Simon.

SIMON. My friends call me Sy.

EVE. Am I a friend?

SIMON. Something like friendship—not quite so innocent. And your name is?

EVE. Eve.

SIMON. Dangerous name. *(Lights a cigarette. Hands one to her.)* Pretty, though.

EVE. Thanks.

SIMON. Feeling better?

EVE. A little.

SIMON. Glad I could help.

EVE. It was wonderful. *(Quiet.)*

SIMON. I feel like I should say something.

EVE. We spent all last night talking.

SIMON. Can you remember what we said?

EVE. Yeah. We were talking about parts of the city and old lovers and how it is to be lonely.

SIMON. And you were saying something about the flowers at your house.

EVE. You complained about not having any more wine. You know, I guess I really don't know what we talked about. Nothing important, I guess.

SIMON. Nothing important?

EVE. Well, nothing conventional. No polite "how do you dos," small talk, background information, that sort of thing. We talked for hours and I still don't know anything about you.

SIMON. I've bared myself to you.

EVE. Yeah, in the literal sense. But how do I know you're not a criminal?

SIMON. Would it bother you if I was?

EVE. Are you?

SIMON. So this is what happens when you skip the pleasantries. No, not exactly.

EVE. What do you do?

SIMON. Eat, sleep, talk, comfort distraught young women who end up lost in my neighborhood, breathe. Occasionally I think.

EVE. Simon, what do you really do?

SIMON. When I'm not giving smartass answers to questions like "What do you do?" I'm a photographer.

EVE. What do you photograph?

SIMON. Whatever I want. Usually city scenes of some kind. Buildings at sunset. People waiting at street corners. I like details.

EVE. And you support yourself doing this?

SIMON. No, but does it matter? I live off odd jobs. Doesn't bother me.

EVE. What about security?

SIMON. How do you mean?

EVE. Oh, you know, what next week will bring, where you'll be in five years. All that jazz.

SIMON. Fuck security.

EVE. You're still drunk.

SIMON. Maybe a little, but I mean that. You see, I'm into accidental flashes. Perpetual motion and rapid change. Things that disappear in seconds. It's why I like the city.

EVE. This is what you photograph, right?

SIMON. Yeah. I take them so I don't have to keep looking for lost moments.

EVE. Lost opportunities.

SIMON. Hell, you miss opportunity, chances are you can pick it up the next time around. Sorta like when you miss your train, and you take a later one. Different passengers, but ultimately the same route.

EVE. So opportunity works like the subway. That's a lousy metaphor.

SIMON. I'm a photographer, what do you want?

EVE. And lost moments are somehow different?

SIMON. Moments pass in the blink of an eye. And then they're gone forever. If you're lucky, you remember how they felt, or smelled or looked. But you can't relive them. So I have my pictures. A nice photo of something long gone. But each moment, no matter how perfect, is gonna end. You can't keep up. And you're going to change. It's just a matter of time. Just like you and your friend last night.

EVE. That was just a sudden reaction. I'm sure in a couple of days...

SIMON. Everything will be back to normal?

EVE. Yeah, I've been with David for almost a year. We know everything about each other. I just got panicked, maybe the food wasn't good, or I had too much on my mind...

SIMON. So you're in love with him?

EVE. Well, I...

SIMON. If you want to marry him, why are you still here?

EVE. Because I...I...well, I...OK, you might have a point.

SIMON. One moment you were somewhere with him and then that moment was over and you were with me.

EVE. Simon's Theory of Moments.

SIMON. You like it? Maybe I should get it copyrighted.

EVE. But, if I buy into it, then I'd have to remember that this moment will be over soon.

SIMON. It's inevitable. Of course, we can let it linger as long as you want.

EVE. But, isn't this a one-night stand?

SIMON. Is it?

EVE. I dunno. I've never had one before. I'm usually pretty careful about things.

SIMON. Secure?

EVE. I didn't say that. Careful. I watch myself. I do try and leave room for the unexpected. This being the unexpected.

SIMON. I guess I should ask what you do.

EVE. I didn't say?

SIMON. No.

EVE. Marketing.

SIMON. Work here in town?

EVE. Out in the suburbs. My dad owns the company. I've been working there for almost four years.

SIMON. Oh.

EVE. We have some really great accounts. The power company. A resort on the coast. Some technical stuff. You probably think this is really boring, don't you?

SIMON. You like it?

EVE. You answer questions with questions. That's annoying. *(Lights cigarette.)* It's a good job, secure. I don't really think about liking it, per se, but changing takes too much effort.

SIMON. Think so?

EVE. Yeah. A lot of hassle. I don't know what else I'd do.

SIMON. Should you ever need any ideas...

EVE. I think you'd be a bad influence.

SIMON. Why is that?

EVE. You seem like the type that would encourage me to abandon stability and run off into the great wide open, live in some bohemian squalor, and never give a shit about what anyone thought of me. Meaning no disrespect of course.

SIMON. Of course.

EVE. And I wouldn't go. I have too much at stake. Couldn't risk it.

SIMON. Eve, you said it.

EVE. Oh.

SIMON. And I would never encourage you to run off into the "great wide open."

EVE. You wouldn't?

SIMON. No way. I'd just try to get you to move downtown.

EVE. Downtown?

SIMON. Yeah, I know this mostly unfurnished apartment that might become available in the near future. Kinda looks like this one.

EVE. I think I know the place.

SIMON. Yeah? *(Kisses her.)*

EVE. What the hell am I doing? Jesus...I've gotta go. *(Slides off bed, starts to pull on clothes.)* I've gotta get home. I...I, I can't find my shoes. Shit...

SIMON. Eve.

EVE. You see them?

SIMON. You don't have to rush off like this.

EVE. Yes I do. I almost lost my... Are they by the bed?

SIMON. No... Eve...

EVE. What?

SIMON. Could I get a picture of you? Just for the moment.

EVE. You ask this of all your conquests?

SIMON. Only a select few.

EVE. So I should be honored.

SIMON. Something like that.

EVE. Do you want me to pose or anything?

SIMON. No, just start walking toward the door. *(EVE walks R.)* Eve. *(She turns. Flash.)* Thanks.

EVE. See you.

SIMON. Hey, if I had really asked you to abandon security and come live in my—what was it?—bohemian squalor, would you have done it? *(Pause. EVE is facing away from him.)*

EVE. Simon, there's no way I could have...

SIMON. Just wondering. It was nice to meet you, Eve.

EVE. My pleasure. *(Turns toward him.)* Goodbye...

(Lights fade on SIMON.)

EVE. And that was pretty much it. I was in a daze walking to the train because it was already sunset again. We'd slept all day and the sky was orange between the buildings and surreal. Took me a minute to remember I had no shoes on and my dress was missing a button and the wind caught up my skirt. I rode home barefoot. You laughed when you picked me up at the train station. Said I looked silly.

BEATRICE. You did.

EVE *(steps out of the shadows)*. I didn't care. It was the perfect moment. *(Walks back. Sits beside BEATRICE.)*

BEATRICE. And you didn't hear from him again.

EVE. Not until one morning several months later. I walked out on my porch on the way to work and found my shoes on the welcome mat, a picture of me with a message on the back.

BEATRICE. What did it say?

EVE. Another moment of your time, please, and his telephone number. But I had already started seeing Ben. I've never told him, you know. Never told him about any of it. I guess it seemed unnecessary. And I've never seen Simon since.

BEATRICE. Probably a good thing.

EVE. But I have been thinking about him an awful lot lately. You know, sometimes I get up in the morning and wander outside and halfway expect to see him standing there waiting to whisk me away and tell me he's been dreaming about me every night for the past year and...

BEATRICE. And you ride off in the sunset and live happily ever after. I think I know this story. And it's a fairy tale.

EVE. I know.

BEATRICE. I wish I believed you did.

EVE. So, dinner at your place, right?

BEATRICE. Right. Henry's cooking. We're throwing our own farewell party. Since none of our good friends have offered...

EVE. You never gave me a chance. Besides, I thought you said the guys that work with Henry were having some kinda bon voyage thing.

BEATRICE. And it was loads of fun, lemme tell you—actually, there's nothing to tell. But I have high hopes that tonight will be a little more exciting.

EVE. I'm sure it will be.

BEATRICE. Till then?

EVE. Bye.

BEATRICE (*walks away, then turns back*). Maybe you should tell him, Eve. Enough time has passed. It doesn't seem quite fair.

EVE. I will. I'm just holding out for the perfect moment.

BEATRICE. Jesus, you are...

EVE. Being completely ridiculous, I know. That's what you've always said.

BEATRICE. You are going to break his heart. That's what I was going to say. (*Blackout.*)

SCENE TWO

SETTING: *EVE's front porch.*

AT RISE: *BEN is smoothing his hair in the window.*

BEN. You ready soon?

(EVE pokes head around the front door.)

EVE. Just a minute. Don't worry. Bea and Henry will hold dinner. They know I'm never on time.

BEN. Do I look OK?

EVE. Stupid question. We're just having dinner. Both of them know you.

BEN. I know, just sometimes I worry...

EVE. About what? The fashion police?

BEN. No, no, that I don't exactly fit into your world.

EVE. That's the most ridiculous thing I've ever heard.

BEN. Your friends are intimidating...

EVE. I don't want to hear any more...

BEN. Like Henry, he's so, set, so...

EVE *(turns to face him)*. He's so "what," Ben?

BEN. You know... *(Quiet.)*

EVE. Do you have a light?

BEN. You're changing the subject.

EVE. Deliberately. Your lighter please. *(BEN hands it to her. EVE lights a cigarette.)* Anyway, they're leaving soon. You won't have to put up with them for much longer.

BEN. Do you ever feel like you're taking some kind of risk being with me?

EVE. Jesus, Ben, do you really think...

BEN. Do you?

EVE. I feel completely safe being with you. Secure, even.

BEN. Good.

EVE. Is it?

BEN. What?

EVE. Never mind. *(Sits on step.)* Why all of this now?

BEN. I've just been thinking.

EVE. Thinking too much. Overanalyzing. Your favorite activity.

BEN. It fills the empty spaces. At least I don't talk to myself, or sing along with the songs on the radio, or... *(He looks over to EVE, who is biting her nails.)* chew on my nails.

EVE. Nervous habit.

BEN. It's kind of cute. Makes you seem vulnerable every now and then. I don't mind.

EVE. Ben, I need to tell you something...

BEN. I think during work, in between phone calls. Have a lot of ideas, you know? I've doodled a million plans for success and five-minute philosophies on the back of paperwork. You never know, if I'm bored for long enough, I might come up with something really profound.

EVE. Ben...

BEN. OK, maybe just slightly profound. Still better than listening to my boss talk about her convict ex-husband in the break room. You'd probably think she was funny—loud and abrasive, yet still fundamentally flaky. Seems like going to work is becoming more and more like one of those human interest movies starring a bunch of nutcases, all with talk-show-style problems. I don't know why I'm still there.

EVE. You're not listening...

BEN. To reason, yeah, I know. I should probably try to find something new. I mean anything would be better, but you know how I get neurotic when it comes to change. And I'm oddly compelled to keep going back. Like, I think one day, something really important might happen. What it is, I don't know.

EVE. Jesus Christ, Ben.

BEN. What?

EVE. You're not listening to me at all. I said I had to tell you something. You just break in and finish my sentences and tell me all your stupid anecdotes. I hate that.

BEN. I'm sorry.

EVE. Can I just say what I set out to say?

BEN. You don't have to.

EVE. Why not?

BEN. I know what you're going to say.

EVE. You do?

BEN. Yeah. You're ashamed of me, right?

EVE. Oh, Ben...

BEN. No, I understand. It's my job, and my life. I can't get my shit together. I sit around talking about trivial work bullshit. Laughing off my knack for bad ideas that never come into fruition, and we've been discussing a serious relationship. I still can't give you the kind of life Henry and Beatrice have, where everything is just in place and beautiful. Not even close.

EVE. I don't believe we're having this conversation.

BEN. I don't mind, Evie, we should talk about these things. I know they bother you.

EVE. Ben, they bother you. Not me. I've told you that a million times.

BEN. Not at all.

EVE. Uh-uh. In fact, it's the thing that bothers me the least. See, this is why all that thinking is bad for you.

BEN. Yeah, I had all these defenses and explanations plotted out, from a bunch of different perspectives. Suggestions.

EVE. Save them for a rainy day. We've gotta go. *(Starts walking back toward the door.)* Ben, if you're so uncomfortable with your life it seems like maybe you should do something. It's time for a change. A progression into something new.

BEN. A progression... Are you reading my mind? *(Looks at watch.)* Pause this conversation. We'll pick up later.

EVE. I really think we should talk...

BEN *(turns back toward EVE).* You look beautiful, sweetie. Were you going to say something?

EVE. I guess it's not important.

BEN. Sure?

EVE. Yeah, yeah it was nothing. Let's go.

BEN *(takes her hand).* OK. *(They exit L. Blackout.)*

SCENE THREE

SETTING: *A table set L. Four chairs.*

AT RISE: *BEATRICE and HENRY are setting plates and silverware.*

BEATRICE. ...you know how Eve is. She sat there and told me all of this just after announcing that she and Ben were getting more serious.

HENRY. Hon, what are you going to do when we live three thousand miles from Eve and her made-for-TV love affairs? How on earth will you pass the time?

BEATRICE. Don't be an ass. I just feel like she needs someone to talk to. It's not like she plans her life to be so absurd.

HENRY. You don't think so? I think she loves it. All the melodrama. Do you realize since I've married you she's been through Ben and David and Jay and Steve and Brad and now this other guy, Simon.

BEATRICE. That's the whole problem. She's not finished with Simon yet. Or Ben. It's like...

HENRY. Are you listening to yourself?

BEATRICE. You're just acting superior because once upon a time she jilted you too.

HENRY. Case closed. And that was after what's-his-name, Andy?

BEATRICE. Chris. Andy came after you.

HENRY. Three thousand miles. A small price to pay for a departure from Eve land.

BEATRICE. I really am excited about going.

HENRY (*puts his arm around her*). So am I. (*Steps away.*) I have to go check on the chicken. (*Walks offstage.*)

BEATRICE. It really is different this time.

HENRY. What?

BEATRICE. Eve. She really has changed, you know. Think about her over the past two years.

HENRY (*walks out with a spoon*). Taste this.

BEATRICE (*takes spoon*). She quit the job working for her father. Started working for that magazine. Started dating Ben, the last person on the face of the planet I would have ever imagined her with. And you know how she's been weird. I haven't seen her wear pastels in months. (*Takes bite.*)

HENRY. Too much curry?

BEATRICE. More salt. (*HENRY walks back onstage.*) I think it might be more significant than you may think...

HENRY. Bullshit.

BEATRICE. Henry, don't be so immature.

HENRY. Immature? Because I can't in all good faith take Eve seriously? Not for five minutes, not for one second. At least not anymore. I've been there, done that, won the consolation T-shirt. And now, five years later I'm married to you, very happy with you, why should I have to worry about her?

BEATRICE. We've been friends forever.

HENRY. Which I respect.

BEATRICE. And she really is quite naive, Henry, you'd be surprised.

HENRY. Oh for Chrissake. *(Doorbell rings.)* Would you get that?

BEATRICE. Yes. Just no more comments. We have to be nice.

HENRY. You started it.

BEATRICE. You know what I mean, Henry.

HENRY. Fine, fine. *(Walks offstage.)*

(BEATRICE walks L, followed back by BEN.)

BEN. Eve left something in the car. She said she'd be back in a minute.

BEATRICE. Well, make yourself comfortable. Henry should have dinner ready soon.

BEN. Smells great. What is it?

BEATRICE. Something exotic I can't pronounce. Involves chicken in some capacity. *(Pulls out a chair.)* Can I get you a drink?

BEN. Sure.

BEATRICE. Beer, wine...

BEN. Do you have any Scotch?

BEATRICE. I think so. Might be packed. *(Walks offstage.)*

BEN. I wanted to thank you again for the books. They're great.

BEATRICE. Don't mention it.

BEN. No really. I haven't read them. I'm not working for the next few days, so I anticipate having a chance to sit down and read. I was feeling a little under the weather today. I need a short sick leave.

(BEATRICE walks onstage.)

BEATRICE. You're sick?

BEN. I'm always sick. I've been feeling worse recently.

BEATRICE. Maybe you should see a doctor.

BEN *(takes sip).* I hate doctors. Too expensive and they never can seem to figure out what's wrong with me.

BEATRICE. Maybe it's all in your head.

BEN. I worry it could be terminal.

(HENRY enters from L.)

HENRY. Ben. Hello. My deepest sympathies, as usual.

BEN. Nice to see you too, Henry. This place looks empty. When are you leaving?

HENRY. Not soon enough.

BEATRICE. Wednesday. Henry wants to drive out, for some unknown reason.

HENRY. See the country, hon. Enjoy America. Both of us have been stuck on the East Coast for entirely too long.

BEATRICE. He wants to see the Grand Canyon.

HENRY. Among other things. What she won't tell you is that we promised to spend three nights with her sister in Arkansas. It's not completely my fool plan.

BEATRICE. We haven't seen Kate since we got married.

HENRY. What the hell reason have we ever had to go to Arkansas before?

BEN. Eve's mother lives out that way, doesn't she? We've always meant to visit.

HENRY. Eve always talks about visiting her mother. To my knowledge, she's never taken anyone out there.

BEN. Well, I think we might have reason to go, sometime soon. We've been talking about something. Don't tell her I said this, but I'm thinking about asking her to...

BEATRICE. Illinois. Eve's mother lives in Illinois. That's not really near Arkansas.

BEN. Oh. *(Doorbell.)*

HENRY. Speak of the devil.

BEATRICE. I'll get it. *(Walks R.)*

HENRY. So, you been watching the playoffs?

(Lights come up C over EVE and BEATRICE.)

BEATRICE. What's wrong?

EVE. I have to tell him. You're right. I can't keep all this secret anymore. It doesn't make any sense.

BEATRICE. Wait. You're going to tell him what...

HENRY. ...So, what was it you wanted to ask me?

BEN. You and Eve. When you were still together, did you ever ask her to marry you?

HENRY. I know I thought about it. Never bought a ring, if that's what you mean. We were still pretty young then, just out of school. Eve was wild. Had a reputation for ending relationships. I don't suppose I wanted to put myself through the rejection.

BEATRICE. ...Are you serious?

EVE. Completely. All I've done all day is think about him. After we talked, I left a message on his answering machine. Asked him to call me. I think I'm in love with him.

BEATRICE. Eve you spent one night with this guy. Almost a year ago.

EVE. It was the best night of my life. And maybe he's been thinking about me, Bea. It's worth a try, at least I'll know.

BEN. ...She's never seemed that way to me.

HENRY. Maybe she's changed. Gotten older. I've certainly changed. Aw hell, I know she's changed. God, over the past year she's almost become a different person.

BEN. Maybe I've had something to do with that.

HENRY. With Eve, anything's possible.

BEATRICE. ...So what exactly are you going to do?

EVE. I dunno. I'm getting tired of living out here. Everything is so clean, so static. I need some movement in my life.

BEATRICE. You'd stay at the magazine?

EVE. For the time being, but I was considering going off in some new direction. I've been thinking about pursuing some artistic project. I'm still young, you know, now would be a good time to do something crazy, maybe move into the city, downtown somewhere.

BEN. ...And I've put aside a little money, Thought maybe she'd like to buy a house somewhere out here.

HENRY. You getting burned out on city life?

BEN. I've never lived anywhere else. It'd be nice to be somewhere quiet and green for a while. Besides, Eve seems to like it out here. She's the kind of girl who appreciates security.

EVE. ...Fuck security. Security has been my credo my whole life. Everybody else gets to be a little insane for a while. I've always been the boring one.

BEATRICE. You've never been the boring one.

EVE. You know what I mean. I just want to throw caution to the wind. It's like I started dating Ben because I thought he'd be different. More reckless, maybe. And the longer I'm with him, the more he becomes just like everyone else...

BEN. ...I've been looking for a new job. Trying to get my shit together.

HENRY. Telephone business got you down?

BEN. It was OK when it was just me, you know? But I can't marry a girl like Eve and do what I do. She's too good for all that. I want to give her a beautiful life. Nice things.

HENRY. Eve has plenty of nice things. Always has.

BEN. I know. But I want to give them to her, I want to take care of her.

EVE. ...You're not listening to me.

BEATRICE. Of course I am, you're talking like a seventeen-year-old girl.

EVE. Is it so wrong to want a little space? I've always had all these other people who took care of me, and now I want to take care of myself. I'm twenty-six years old, Bea, it's about fucking time, don't you think?

BEATRICE. Ssh. Quiet down. Fine, fine, so what are you going to do? Just walk away from your life?

EVE. I figure I'll just take the summer, work in the city, doing whatever, find a place, see if it works. I have to do it now, otherwise, I'm going to lose my moment.

BEN. ...Come summer, I think I'll rent a place on the beach for a few days. Thought I might take her down there, sit on the beach, be romantic and stupid...

BEATRICE. ...But you haven't even talked to Simon.

EVE. He'll understand, I know. The opportunity is presenting itself again, and I know he'll...

BEATRICE. You don't even know his last name.

EVE. What's that supposed to mean?

BEATRICE. You're back in the fairy tale again, Eve. This is not the way life works.

EVE. No, but don't you see, he was the one who helped me understand. It was his idea, almost.

BEATRICE. His fault.

EVE. What did you say?

BEATRICE. Nothing. *(Touches EVE's shoulder.)* We've been friends for a long time. I've watched you make thousands...

EVE. Bea...

BEATRICE. Thousands of mistakes...

HENRY. ...Oh, Ben.

BEN *(putting ring box back in his pocket)*. Too much?

HENRY. Oh shit, Ben.

BEN. What? At least tell me if I'm on the right track.

BEATRICE. ...Eve, what are you going to do when I'm not three blocks away to hold your hand when the world comes crashing down on you again?

HENRY. ...Food's getting cold, Why don't you tell the ladies to come in now?

BEN (stands). I'm going to prove you wrong. (Walks to BEATRICE and EVE.) Dinner's ready.

EVE. How long have you been standing there?

BEN. Just got here. Come sit down. Whatever Henry's made smells great. (Pulls her beside the table.) You look beautiful.

EVE. Thanks. (He kisses her.) What was that for?

BEN. I missed you.

EVE. You saw me ten minutes ago.

BEN. Still, I missed you.

EVE. Silly. (BEN pulls out her chair. EVE, HENRY, and BEATRICE sit.)

BEATRICE. Henry, if you'll pour the wine.

HENRY (pours). The last bottle unpacked for your pleasure.

BEN (to EVE). You doing OK?

EVE. Fine. I'm fine. Just have a lot on my mind right now.

HENRY. I'd like to make a toast. To changing directions and new locations.

EVE. To the perfect moment.

BEATRICE. To happiness and security.

BEN. To those we love. (They clink glasses and drink.)

SCENE FOUR

SETTING: The same.

AT RISE: A couple of hours later. EVE, BEATRICE, HENRY, and BEN are still sitting at the table, dishes cleared. EVE, HENRY, and BEN are smoking.

HENRY. I promised Bea I would quit when we moved. It's been a bad habit for long enough. And I have enough bad habits without this one.

BEATRICE. I'll believe it when I see it.

HENRY. Believe it. This time I'm dead serious. Besides, rumor has it they're not so tobacco friendly out there. It'll give me good incentive to quit.

BEATRICE. I was never enough incentive.

HENRY. You were fine, I just had these two around all the time. *(Points to BEN and EVE.)*

BEN. Don't try to pin the blame on me.

HENRY. You, my friend, smoke like a locomotive. How could I possibly expect to behave myself with you single-handedly keeping some tobacco companies in business?

BEATRICE. Self-control?

HENRY. She nags. This, Ben, is what marriage will do to you.

BEN. Eve's not much of a complainer. Are you, hon?

EVE. Please stop.

BEATRICE. So, Eve, what have you been working on recently?

EVE. Nothing important.

BEATRICE. Work OK?

EVE. Fine.

BEATRICE. I noticed you started working on your flowers. They look lovely.

EVE. Waste of time. There's supposed to be a front tonight. They'll probably die.

BEATRICE. Ben, anything new in your life?

BEN. I've been working all the time. Started building bookcases in my living room, but I'm a real klutz with a hammer.

HENRY. Eve's always had a knack for projects. She likes to build things.

BEN. Really? *(To EVE.)* You never told me.

HENRY. Yeah, build things, clean things up, tear 'em down, isn't that right, babe?

BEATRICE. Henry. *(Slaps him lightly.)* He's had a little too much to drink.

HENRY *(to BEN)*. Ask her, kiddo. I'm sure she'd be glad to help.

BEN. Evie, you never told me...

EVE. Don't, Ben.

BEN. Don't what?

EVE. First of all, don't call me Evie, it's juvenile and it drives me crazy. And, Henry, I think you can let it go, now.

HENRY. What? I've tread on sacred ground now, hon? I'm leaving town in three days and I won't have a chance to give you the shit you deserve for quite a while. It's only fair.

BEATRICE. Henry, stop.

EVE. I haven't done anything to you, Henry. We broke up over five years ago. I'm sure Beatrice is much better for you than I ever was.

HENRY. She's twice the woman you are. *(To BEN.)* Listen and learn, kid, you'll need this sooner than you think. *(To EVE.)* Tell me, now that you have this one in the palm of your hand, how long before you crush him?

BEATRICE. Shut up, Henry. *(To BEN.)* Don't listen to him...

HENRY. How long? *(Points to BEN.)* He's not gonna have the balls to say any of this to you. So you might as well listen to me.

EVE. Henry, this has long since been appropriate subject for our conversation...

HENRY. Have you already been unfaithful to him? Or are you just waiting for the right moment?

EVE. The right...

HENRY. He's already remade his life for you. And you're finished with him. And I have reason to believe you've already found your next target.

EVE. Bea, did you tell him?

BEATRICE. I just said...

BEN. What's going on here, I don't understand.

HENRY. It's funny, although I don't care anymore, I feel like I have some right to know. And he... *(Points to BEN.)* he certainly has some right to know.

BEN. What is he talking about?

EVE. If you'll just give me a chance...

HENRY. Tell him, tell him right now.

BEATRICE. Stop it, Henry.

HENRY. What are you talking about? You're the one who told me all of this. You agree with me. Why the hell are you siding with her?

BEATRICE. Fucking shit, Henry, will you please stop now?

HENRY. Tell him, Eve. Now you've gotten me stuck in your soap opera and I can't wait to see how this episode ends.

BEN. Eve.

EVE. I have to go.

HENRY. Leave, good, go. Have a nice trip.

BEN. Eve.

EVE. Shut up, Ben. *(To HENRY.)* Henry, this has nothing to do with you. Nothing. You have a different life. I have a different life. Enough. I'm leaving. *(Turns and walks R.)*

HENRY. And she leaves so cool, so calm, avoiding as always the big scene...

EVE. You son of a bitch. *(Turns to HENRY.)* You wanna know why I left you? Why I left you five fucking years ago...

HENRY. Because you could. Because I couldn't say this shit to you then. Because I was like him. *(Points to BEN.)* Some fucking stupid, blind asshole, who let you drag me through shit whenever you felt like being the bitch you are. And then when you reached your point of fulfillment, you got bored and dropped me. And left me wondering why I wasn't fucking good enough for you. So I changed.

EVE. Into a drunken shithead?

HENRY. You'd love to blame this on my weakness.

EVE. I hate you.

HENRY. You made me this way. And I hope you never forget that.

EVE. Bea, I am truly sorry for you. *(To HENRY.)* You haven't changed, Henry. You're still the same ignorant dick you were once upon a fucking time. I still think you're pathetic, and I will always be too goddamn good for you.

HENRY. Go to hell.

EVE. Fuck you. *(She walks R.)*

HENRY. Eve, I hope he breaks your heart. Crushes you into a million pieces. And I don't say that for me. I'm happy now. I'm fine now. I say that for all the others. Those whose names I can't even remember, and for this one, whose name you won't remember in six months. I say that because you need it. I say that because I won't be around to see it happen. *(EVE exits.)*

BEN. Eve, wait... *(Silence.)*

HENRY. I have to go out for a while.

BEATRICE. OK. *(Lights fall on BEATRICE alone.)*

SCENE FIVE

SETTING: *Front porch.*

AT RISE: *Late night. A little while later. EVE is sitting on the steps, frantically dialing and redialing a number into a portable phone. Audience hears faint busy signals. Enter BEN from L.*

BEN. That you?

EVE *(puts the phone down, wipes her face)*. Yeah, Ben, right here. *(She stands. BEN goes to embrace her but she steps away, up the stairs.)* Have a seat.

BEN *(sits)*. I suppose we should talk.

EVE. Ben, I hope you weren't taking Henry too seriously.

BEN. Henry was drunk. I left right after you did.

EVE. Go home?

BEN. No. It's too far to ride home and come back. I just wandered around the neighborhood, watched the stars, had a drink at the corner of Hemphill. Scared the shit out of some kids playing vandal in some front yard.

EVE. What were they doing?

BEN. It was dark. I couldn't really tell, but I think they were trying to spray-paint some poor dog.

EVE *(laughs, slides onto the porch railing, back against column)*. You do stupid shit when you're young, I guess. Do you have a cigarette?

BEN. Sure. *(Hands her one. Stands to light it and sits down again.)*

EVE. Crazy dinner party.

BEN. Yeah. *(Lights a cigarette.)* Do you know what time it is?

EVE. No, I don't wear a watch. *(A church chimes three from the distance.)*

BEN. I guess that answers my question. Maybe I should leave.

EVE. I don't care, You can go whenever you want. It's not like I'll turn into a pumpkin.

BEN. It's kinda cold out here.

EVE. You're always cold.

BEN. Life is cold. Just flat reality and then we die.

EVE. You're such a cliché.

BEN. Am I?

EVE. You brood a lot. Take things too seriously. Tell people your aesthetic is sadness.

BEN. Only once, and I was just kidding around.

EVE. It was my father, Ben.

BEN. And that makes me a cliché?

EVE. For who you are, yes... I do miss summer though.

BEN. I thought you hated warm weather.

EVE. I don't like it when it gets overhot. Sticky, one hundred percent humidity, and I end up stuck in five o'clock traffic behind a bunch of tourists in minivans. I do like warm things, though. Sunlight on my back. Sunsets at nine o'clock, when the sky turns crazy colors.

BEN. You know I never get to see the sunset. I work straight through it. We've never watched one together.

EVE. No.

BEN. I'd like to.

EVE. They've been nice recently. Really red.

BEN. Maybe I'll take that vacation come summer. We'll go to the coast. Watch sunsets. Sit on the sand. Last summer I went to this little place—you'd love it—this cottage with some friends from town, had a wonderful time.

EVE. I didn't go anywhere.

BEN (walks to railing). I didn't know you last summer.

EVE. I didn't know anybody. Particularly people like you. I was usually lonely.

BEN. You've changed a lot. I can't help but feel responsible.

EVE. Don't give yourself too much credit. It was my decision. You were not the catalyst.

BEN (touches her face). You're beautiful.

EVE. You're crazy.

BEN. Crazy in love with you, despite it all.

EVE. Hmm. A sudden gush of affection. That's unexpected.

BEN. You know you could never get rid of me.

EVE. Even though I live way out here and you're in town and we're totally incongruous together?

BEN. Despite all that. Didn't you hear me the first time. I love you regardless. You just keep changing and I'm trying to get used to it.

EVE. I don't change all that often. You make me sound superficial.

BEN. No, you just keep turning into something I don't understand. I try, but every time I see you you're more and more...

EVE. You just didn't know anything about me before. I'm not changing that fast. People like Henry make you see me a different way.

BEN. Fuck Henry. That's not what I'm talking about. You're more and more...

EVE. More what?

BEN. Who was it?

EVE. Who was who?

BEN. The catalyst from before. The one who made you change.

EVE. I don't know. Maybe it wasn't a person at all.

BEN. You were changing when I met you.

EVE. I guess I was.

BEN. What started it? I'm curious.

EVE. That's just it. Curiosity. I didn't understand the way I was anymore. I just changed it. Don't you ever want to do that? Just tell yourself to change and do it?

BEN. Seems like a waste of time. The least I can do is just accept things as being the way they are. Make it flow till it's done.

EVE. So you live to die?

BEN. Don't we all?

EVE. Maybe. But I can't see the need for making the inevitable any easier. "Flow till it's done"? Do you spend time thinking up this shit?

BEN. You're just naive.

EVE. Far, far from the truth. You, dear, are a cynic.

BEN. Not quite. You don't seem to realize you're all that makes my life worthwhile. In some sense I live my life for you.

EVE. Your devotion embarrasses me. I'm not worth it. There are so many other things...

BEN (starts pacing). Not for me. Eve, I really don't have anything. Most of my friendships are superficial. My family life is nonexistent. I'm not overly talented or overly intellectual. All I know is what we have and what we've had has been the only part of my life that hasn't been a mistake. I have faith in you, you know. I know you will always see niceness when I can't.

EVE. Niceness or niceties?

BEN. Niceness. I'm beyond niceties.

EVE. Hardly. (Stands.) You love saying shit like that, you know?

BEN. Just to irritate you.

EVE. Just to make yourself feel better. I think you like playing the tragic hero too much. Hamlet with a twist?

BEN. Sounds like a cocktail. "Yes, I'd like a Hamlet with a twist on the rocks. And could I have one of those little umbrellas, please?"

EVE. You can be funny every now and then. I don't require that you always keep so damned serious.

BEN. Thanks for telling me.

EVE. Your pacing is making me nervous.

BEN. I've been unhappy most of my life. Things go to shit on me, and I don't usually understand why.

EVE. Misery is a drug, Ben. And you are an addict.

BEN. You don't understand. I mean, you live in a context without unhappiness.

EVE. Just your perception. I have it in me to be every bit as miserable as you think you are.

BEN. You don't understand.

EVE. I heard you the first time. *(Grabbing his arm.)* Stop pacing, goddammit, you're making me dizzy.

BEN *(stops)*. Sorry.

EVE *(returns to her seat)*. You don't have to be sorry. Just stop. *(Pause.)* You are not so bad off. It's all in your head.

BEN. Eve ... what Henry said ...

EVE. Henry's a drunk, you said so yourself, and I don't want to talk about it. I think it's time for you to tell me one of those anecdotes.

BEN. OK, once I was at this dinner party, and this guy, whose life is near perfect, starts insulting my girlfriend out of nowhere. I'm too confused to defend her, because I don't understand why he's saying what he's saying, or why it comes out then. But mostly what I don't understand is how my girlfriend could stand to be with me, when she says this guy will never be good enough for her.

EVE. You might have taken it as a compliment, Ben. And Henry's life obviously isn't perfect. It just looks good on paper.

BEN. But it's secure.

EVE. Yeah? Well, love doesn't have a damn thing to do with security. Not that kind of security, anyway. *(Quiet. Wind chimes play. BEN removes ring box from pocket, tosses it around, then opens it toward EVE.)*

BEN. Will you marry me?

EVE. Jesus, what?

BEN. Will you marry me?

EVE. That came out of nowhere.

BEN. No, it didn't, Eve. We've been heading this way for a while. I was gonna wait until I got myself in a better place, but to hell with it. It doesn't matter anyway, then I think now is as good a time as any.

EVE. Ben, I don't know what...

BEN. Look, I had to get it out, say the words. From here on out, it should be easy, right? You have one of two answers, whatever you say, I'll live with it. We'll live through it. I just had to...

EVE. This is such a complicated time. You should have waited.

BEN. Why? Keep all of it inside me, laugh off everything we've done? When better than right now? Late at night, with the stars out, after that terrible dinner, and you're sitting beside me, so close. I love you, Eve. I had to take this moment. This is the perfect moment.

EVE *(rapidly walks away)*. Shit.

BEN. You OK?

EVE. No... Yeah, you just reminded me of someone.

BEN. Who?

EVE. You don't know him?

BEN. Who is he?

EVE. Someone from last summer.

BEN. Someone you were involved with?

EVE. Kind of.

BEN. You're not making any sense.

EVE. It was a one-night stand. In the city.

BEN. My city.

EVE. You've claimed possession. How arrogant. Yes, your city. Is there another one?

BEN. Not here.

EVE. I don't think you know his part of the city.

BEN. I know the city.

EVE. You don't know everything. You don't need to. Just...just understand that he is what you're not.

BEN. Rich, powerful, handsome, content, right? What am I leaving out?

EVE. You really don't listen to me, do you?

BEN. Were you in love with him?

EVE. I was affected by him...

BEN. The catalyst?

EVE. Partly, but I don't want you to get the idea I changed just for him.

BEN. Have you seen him since?

EVE. Don't you mean to ask me if I've seen him since we've been together?

BEN. Well have you?

EVE. I'd rather not answer.

BEN. That's not fair.

EVE. What do you want? An admission of infidelity? He has a habit of showing up from time to time, when I least expect it, in the middle of those mindless, monotonous days you were talking about.

BEN. Why are you hurting me like this?

EVE. You asked me, remember?

BEN. Christ.

EVE. Don't be this way. He's nothing like you at all.

BEN. Is that supposed to make me feel better?

EVE. Well, you can't compete.

BEN. What is he like?

EVE. Please don't ask me any more. He's not here, hasn't been for a while.

BEN. But you're still changing, which if what you say is true, means you must be thinking about him.

EVE. I think about a lot of people, Ben. That's not the same thing as fucking them. You're acting like a child.

BEN. How am I supposed to act?

EVE. Don't act. Accept. It's just the way things are.

BEN. What's happening, Eve?

EVE. I'm changing again. I'm moving toward him. Maybe becoming more like him. Funny thing is, the more distance I gain, the closer I get to him.

BEN. We have a regular triangle now.

EVE. You could say that. I guess I'm still wondering about the exact position of you and I. What we ever were, what we will become, what five years can do. Down the road, you know?

BEN. You're leaving me.

EVE. No, I'm just letting you know that I'm still changing like I was before, and when I finish I don't think you'll understand me at all anymore.

BEN. Are you going to start seeing him?

EVE. Not yet. (*BEN drops his head in his hands. EVE touches his face.*) Stop. I don't want you to do this. Please understand. I don't like to hurt anyone.

BEN. Eve, I would do anything for you. I would be anything for you.

EVE. You do too much.

BEN. You can't leave me. You're all I have. I have nothing else I need like you. You're the only meaning. Alone, I don't know if I can...keep...

EVE. I know I didn't hear that.

BEN. I'm serious. So serious. My life is nothing...I...

EVE. Don't say this. Don't say this, dammit. It will just piss me off and make me feel guilty.

BEN. I love you...Eve...don't...

EVE. I have to, Ben.

BEN. Goddammit, Eve, you can't fucking leave me.

EVE. Try to understand, Ben, please. I can't marry you. You're too good to me.

BEN. I can't understand you. I can't fucking stand here and listen to this...

EVE. I shouldn't leave you.

BEN. Nobody will ever love you the way I do. Nobody else would even want to.

EVE. Will you listen, Ben, will you just...

BEN. You'll never know what you've lost...and I think I've heard enough. *(He exits R.)*

EVE. Ben... Dammit, Ben, come back... Ben... Wait. Ben...Ben... *(She sits, and dials numbers into the phone. The audience hears rings. On the third ring, the curtain falls.)*

END

UPRIGHT

James Hilburn
University of Kansas

CHARACTERS

PAINT: A homeless man in his early 50s.

PELF: A homeless man in his early 20s.

LOPEZ: A tough-looking man in his late 20s. Racial makeup should be of no importance.

UPRIGHT was first produced by the University of Kansas English Alternative Theater on October 9, 1997 in Lawrence, Kan., with the following cast:

Paint .... KARL RAMBERG
Pelf .... MATT CHAPMAN
Lopez........................... AVI SEAVER

Directed by Jeremy Auman; Michelle Dowdy assistant directed, stage managed, and inspired; set design was by Phillip John Schroeder; lighting design was by Michael Senften; props were by Barb Downing, Judith Scheff, and Sandy Clanton; Michelle Dowdy, Laura Graham, Dan Kulmala, Gavan Laessig, Michael Murphy, Kim Wada, and Ed White crewed and assisted.

This play would not have existed without the direction and guidance of Paul Stephen Lim.

The playwright would like to thank: Brent Puglisi (for all of the stories); David Ryan, Rick Watts, Carson Elrod, Hypothetical 7, Ron and Ann Marie Adams; my brothers: Matt, Ryan, and Andrew; Blair Bitters, Portland, Pat Hilburn, and everyone at the Bourgeois Pig.

UPRIGHT

AT RISE: *Five a.m. Beneath an overpass. PAINT enters DR. He is dressed warmly and is pushing a grocery cart filled with items. When he reaches C, he pulls out a coffee can and Sterno from the cart and sets it up to make coffee. PELF enters DR, but cannot be seen by PAINT. He is dressed in a worn leather jacket and jeans, and at the beginning of the play, he should have a damaged hand. He pulls a dark-colored ski mask from his jacket pocket and puts it on. He watches as PAINT pulls items from his cart and sets up camp. As PAINT fishes something out of the cart, PELF steps into the open. He growls like a dog and then barks.*

PELF. Rrrrrrroof. Roof. Roof.

PAINT. What the hell? *(PELF tackles PAINT. They wrestle briefly until PAINT grabs a weapon from the cart and stands over PELF.)*

PELF. Wait, wait. Don't hit. It's me, Pelf. *(PAINT unmasks him.)* See?

PAINT. Hold on a second. *(He pulls a pair of glasses out of his coat pocket.)* Well, Goddamn. I thought I got away from all of you crazy people.

PELF *(laughs).* It's me. Nothing to worry about. Yay! Ha ha. You made it. The cops didn't get you. Wow, they tried to put me in the shelter, but you know what? I got away. Yeah, I ran fast. Can I have some coffee?

PAINT. It's kind of old, but it's warm. *(He pours himself a cup and then fishes an extra one for PELF.)*

PELF. Thanks. Yeah, I ran real fast, you should've seen me ...

PAINT (*pointing to PELF's wounded hand*). Looks like something bit you.

PELF. Oh, yeah. That's from Sweetie, that guy who works for Lopez. Me and him got into it right before the cops came.

PAINT. Here, let me see it. (*Puts his glasses on and looks at it. He fetches a piece of cloth from the cart and begins to dress it.*)

PELF. Those cops sure cleaned up Oldtown. They even got Lopez. Yeah, I saw it. Lopez was ... OUCH!

PAINT. Hold still.

PELF. Lopez was fighting one of them, but the cop wouldn't take it. He just, SMACK, right in his face, knocked him down. I saw it. But I bet Lopez won't go to jail. He wasn't really fighting that hard, and I saw him drop his stuff. Those cops won't find it. Yeah, but I got away. This one cop grabbed me and I was right near Lopez, and then I pretended to be good and helpful. And when Lopez got hit, he let go of me, and I ran.

PAINT. And here you are.

PELF. Yeah, here I am. I heard you went this way, and here I am.

PAINT (*finishing PELF's hand*). And there you go.

PELF. Thanks. Feels better.

PAINT. You should stay away from Lopez and his buddies, you could get yourself killed.

PELF. Yeah, yeah I know. Hey, how did you get your cart all the way up here from Oldtown?

PAINT. A real pain in the ass, but I pulled it.

PELF. You get it from the Safeway on Foster Road?

PAINT. Somewhere near there.

PELF. Wow, you lucked out. You got a good cart. Look, the wheels all work and there's no big holes in it.

PAINT. Wait a minute. Who told you I came out this way?

PELF. Huh?

PAINT. Who told you I came out here? Because I left early in the morning, and I didn't talk to anybody.

PELF. Oh you know. Uh, that one lady.

PAINT. What lady?

PELF. The lady who sleeps out in front of the Buick dealership.

PAINT. You followed me out here.

PELF. Come on...

PAINT. What in the hell do you want?

PELF. I...I was just scared, and I saw the tracks from your cart. And I wanted to see how you were.

PAINT. Pelf, I don't have anything for you. No money. No booze. I don't have anything, so whatever it is you want, the answer is no.

PELF. Look, I brought you something. (*Reaches into his pants pocket.*) Here, look at this. (*PAINT pulls out his glasses and inspects it.*) See. It's Lopez's front tooth. The cop knocked it out of his mouth when he hit him. Yeah, and then after all of the trouble, I went back and Lopez was gone and this was on the ground where he fell. Here, take it. It's good luck. It means that you have his power. You have something up on him. (*He pulls a piece of colorful wrapping paper from PAINT's cart, wraps the tooth, and places it in the cart.*) Here, put it in your cart.

PAINT. I don't know, Pelf.

PELF. Just leave it in the cart. Keep it in there.

PAINT. I don't have anything to trade you for this.

PELF. My present to you. You gave me coffee and fixed my hand.

PAINT. What happens when Lopez comes back and finds out that you gave me his tooth?

PELF. You can't tell him.

PAINT. I don't want to get involved in your mess with Lopez. Seems like everyone he talks to winds up beaten into the ground or dead. And all I need is Mr. Lopez coming out here to talk to me about his missing tooth.

PELF. He won't come here. You found a real nice place.

PAINT. Yeah, this is a nice place. But you've got to be careful. I can't stay here long, because it looks like the kind of neighborhood where people call the police. This is the good part of town. Look, there's even a little park over there. *(Points offstage.)*

PELF. I won't stay here too long. I just need one thing... Oh, come on...I just need your cart.

PAINT. No.

PELF. But your cart is from the Safeway on Foster Road. If I turn it in, I get fifty dollars. You could go steal it back again in a few days.

PAINT. Who would give you fifty dollars for a cart?

PELF. The man at Safeway says he will give me two dollars for every missing cart I bring back. And if I bring back twenty-five carts, I get fifty dollars.

PAINT. You're not getting my cart. The wheels don't wobble and it's real sturdy.

PELF. Paint, I need the fifty dollars. You are the last Safeway cart I can find.

PAINT. Do you know how hard it was pulling it up here?

PELF. Come on, I'm your friend...

PAINT. This is *my* cart, you understand that?

PELF. Don't make me get mean! I gave you something really cool.

PAINT. You gave me some crazy killer guy's tooth.

PELF. Damn it. You're making me mad.

PAINT. What are you going to do? Fight me?

PELF. For fifty dollars?... Yeah! *(He goes for the cart.)*

PAINT *(grabbing the cart and pulling it from the other side).* You're getting silly. Don't make me have to teach you a lesson. *(PELF tips the cart over.)* Look what you did... *(PAINT goes for PELF.)*

PELF. Wait... I didn't mean... *(A police siren is heard.)* Oh shit! *(They stop fighting and run for cover.)* What the hell's going on?

PAINT. Shut up.

PELF *(walks out from hiding).* Nothing. He didn't see us.

PAINT. Get back here, idiot.

PELF. I think he caught a guy speeding.

PAINT. He's going to see you.

PELF. No. He's looking the other way.*(PELF flips the policeman off.)* ASSHOLE!

PAINT. Good, I don't need that shit. OK, now take your scrawny ass and get out of here. Trying to take my cart.

PELF. I like it here. *(He pulls out a pack of cigarettes, takes one, lights it and sits down. PAINT lifts the cart back up and puts the things back in that have fallen out.)*

PAINT. Maybe you didn't hear what I said. You had better take off, because I seriously don't need the kind of shit you bring. So, go! Get out of here.

PELF. OK. OK. *(He moves across the stage, removes his coat, and sits on it.)*

PAINT. What are you doing?

PELF. This is my spot. I claim it for me.

PAINT. This is my bridge.

PELF. Bullshit. You can't have your own bridge. Nobody has their own bridge in Oldtown. Everybody shares.

PAINT. Get the hell out of here. *(PELF remains seated.)* Now. *(PELF blows cigarette smoke at him.)* Why are you doing this? You want me to come over and mess you up, don't you?

PELF. Paint, you aren't going to mess me up. You love the attention. Admit it. You're just a lonely old guy sitting up in his cave waiting for trouble to come out and pay him a visit.

PAINT. Stupid shit. What are you going to do with the fifty dollars?

• PELF. I'm saving up for something.

PAINT. More drugs.

PELF. I don't need drugs right now.

PAINT. Liar.

PELF. I don't need drugs, because of Lopez. *(He reaches into his jacket pocket and pulls out a cloth bag.)* When he heard the cop sirens, Lopez ditched his stash. And I saw where he did. And I came back, and just before I got his tooth, I got his bag. Yay!

PAINT. You are so dead.

PELF. He won't find me, because I will be gone.

PAINT. With just fifty dollars?

PELF. I can buy a bus ticket to Wyoming.

PAINT. Oh. And live off what? Drugs?

PELF. I don't know. Wait a minute, I know what I'll do ... Remember that guy from Atlanta? The short guy with real long red hair? Yeah. He stole a lady's credit card one time, and bought two tickets to Hawaii. Remember? And he took his buddy to Hawaii. I could do that. I could live on the beach in Hawaii, and I'd take you with me.

PAINT. Once Lopez gets out of the lockup, he's gonna know that someone took his stuff. And I know how you shoot your mouth off. You're as good as dead.

PELF. That's why I'm crashing here with you. Come on ... just think about it, Hawaii ...

PAINT. Hawaii.

PELF. And a plane ride, and free food on the plane. We can scam drinks. All we need is to find some old lady. But don't worry. I'll mug her, you just watch out for ...

PAINT. Cut it out.

PELF. Or a jogger. A jogger will be better. A rich jogger will have more money. You push him over and I'll take the cash.

PAINT. That's crazy. Now, you're not going to stay here if I hear any more of this bullshit about Hawaii, or stealing from old ladies, or stealing grocery carts. I don't need trouble.

PELF. OK, OK, you're right. I won't stay here long. I just need to chill out for a minute. It's still hairy in Oldtown and I don't want to go back just yet. Let me smoke one more cigarette and I swear I'll go. *(He lights another cigarette.)* I wouldn't mind hitting a jogger. Who's chasing them? Why are they running? I think I'll chase one someday just to give them a reason for running.

PAINT. You'll find a lot of joggers over there. Joggers are always running through that park.

PELF. I should dress up like a jogger.

PAINT. Like a jogger?

PELF. Yeah, so that I could rob somebody. And then I could run away and nobody would be suspicious of me. Joggers are always running. I could get a pair of sweatpants, easy.

PAINT. Are you stupid? Nobody wears sweatpants anymore when they jog. That would totally give you away. You'd have to get a pair of those tight little running shorts.

PELF. It's still a good idea, though.

PAINT. Knowing you, you'd probably try to mug some really strong guy and he'd kick your ass.

PELF. Or an old lady and she'd hit me with her purse.

PAINT. It would serve you right, you bastard.

PELF. I just need to get away from this town and all of these problems. Hey, can I have some more coffee?

PAINT. I only have a little. So, you get half of a little.

PELF. That's OK. Hey, the big scarf.

PAINT. What?

PELF. I was just looking at your big scarf.

PAINT. What about it?

PELF. I was just looking at it. It looks warm. Comfortable. Can I have it?

PAINT. No.

PELF. I mean, can I look at it? (*PAINT hands him the scarf.*) Did you get it from the clothes dumpster? It's a good find if you did.

PAINT. Somebody gave it to me.

PELF. Tell me the story. C'mon, you tell great stories. I hope someday that you'll put me in one of your stories. I think that would be the best thing in the world. Even better than being famous, because you make people sound important.

PAINT. Shit. OK, I got the scarf a few years back. I was working at this sandwich shop in Oldtown, just cleaning up every once in a while. The guy who owned it ran it himself for about fifty years. He was this tough old World War II bastard. Then one day he decides he's gonna retire and close down the shop. So he gets this idea to sell all of his stock at half price and give away free hot dogs. He gets all of the employees together, including me, and we gathered up everything: food, magazines, beer. We marked everything for half price. And people came. They didn't care that this store was closing down. They just wanted stuff for cheap. It was a busy day, and I must have handed out a million hot dogs. After five o'clock, business dies down. People are all going home from work. So me and this guy are sweeping up. The old man is behind the register counting the money we made, when the door busts open and two guys wearing ski masks run in and yell, "Give us the money." The old man yells back, "Fuck you." So one of the robbers shoots the guy I'm working with. I'm thinking that we're all gonna die, but the old man just looks at them real cool and all and says, "Go ahead and kill them, I don't give a shit. Just means I don't have to pay them tomorrow." One of the crooks turns his gun on me, and I just close my eyes. I was pretty sure I was gonna die. Then I hear this loud "Wham," and the old guy starts swearing. When I finally open my eyes, I see a dead robber in front of me and blood everywhere. The old man had pulled out a gun and shot him, but the other one got away. He told me he couldn't pay me because the guy who escaped took the cash register. So instead, I got a bunch of left-over hot dogs, some beer, and this scarf. It's real nice and comfortable, but you know what?

PELF. What?

PAINT. He told me later that he pulled it off that dead guy. Is that some fucked-up shit or what?

PELF. Really? (*PAINT pulls out a bottle of whiskey and takes a swig.*) Bullshit!

PAINT (*laughing*). Grandmother.

PELF. Awwww man.

PAINT. Christmas.

PELF. I need to get me a scarf like yours.

PAINT. Yeah, you should.

PELF. So, when you die, can I have your scarf?

PAINT. Sure.

PELF. Can I have your cart? I'm your friend. I come out to see you. Nobody else does. But I do, right? You should give me the cart too.

PAINT. You're not getting the cart.

PELF. Why not? You can't keep it if you're dead, and you wouldn't want it to go to just anybody.

PAINT. I'm taking it with me. The cart goes wherever I go. Besides, if I give it to you, Lopez will just take it away.

PELF. Lopez.

PAINT. I'm not going to get rid of you, am I?

PELF. Nope.

PAINT. So then, give me a smoke. *(PELF gives him one. PAINT lights it and sits next to PELF.)*

PELF. How's that?

PAINT. It's a smoke. A smoke's a smoke.

PELF. A smoke's a smoke.

PAINT. You know, most of the time you can be a real pain in the ass.

PELF. I know.

PAINT. Watch out for yourself. I mean really. I think you've put yourself into a bad situation here with Lopez.

PELF. You gonna help me?

PAINT. I'll do what I can. I'm an old man, can't do too much.

PELF. You could give me the cart.

PAINT. OK, Mr. Pain-in-the-ass. I give you the cart, you sell it and get fifty dollars. Now what do you do?

PELF. Buy a bus ticket to Wyoming.

PAINT. Where in Wyoming?

PELF. The cheapest place I can find. I don't have a specific town in mind.

PAINT. That's good, because if you knew where you were going, it would be easier for Lopez to find you.

PELF. So, I guess I'm doing fine.

PAINT. What will you do in Wyoming?

PELF. I'll do what I do here.

PAINT. Nothing.

PELF. Are you trying to bring me down?

PAINT. I'm trying to be practical. You have to think about your life and what you're going to do. Otherwise you just float.

PELF. Look who's talking. And what wonderful things have you done with your life today?

PAINT. Hey. I'm a different story. I have nowhere to go and nowhere to be. I can't handle a regular job, but I've tried.

PELF. You're bringing me down. I want to hear about Max's dog.

PAINT. I've told you that story a million times.

PELF. So what. I like it. It'll get my mind off all the bad things in life. C'mon, Max found that dog somewhere in...

PAINT. In Grant Park.

PELF. Yeah.

PAINT. Grant Park around Christmas, and Max was getting sick.

PELF. The D.T.'s.

PAINT. But he found that dog, or that dog found him, and it just followed him around. After a few weeks he realized that he could hardly take care of himself, let alone the dog, so he tried to get rid of him. He didn't even name him because he knew he couldn't keep him.

PELF. But he couldn't get rid of him.

PAINT. No, he couldn't. That dog really liked Max for some reason. He stuck by him even when Max tried to shake him off. He gave me the dog, but it ran away first chance it got and went to find Max. He even put the dog on the train going downtown, thinking some transit worker would take it to the pound or some animal lover would take him home. But a couple of days later, while Max and I were walking through Midtown, up came that goddamn dog...his tongue hanging out and his bug eyes all happy, tail wagging, looking like he owned the whole damn street. I told Max, "He thinks you're more his dog than he is yours." And, man, Max looked as if he'd start crying. Right then he named that poor damned little dog. He called him...

PELF. Lucky, because he was lucky nobody stepped on him, he was so little.

PAINT. Yeah, Lucky, because nobody stepped on him or took him to the pound. Anyway, Lucky was Max's "for good" dog and he went everywhere with him. Lucky didn't care that Max didn't have a place to live. They both ate the same food, whatever they could scrounge up, and Max kept him tied to his cart. Even though Max was sick, he took good care of that dog.

PELF. Yeah, but then...

PAINT. I'm getting to that part. Max would take him around town, and he taught him to beg for money. One day at the bus station after a slow day of not getting any money, Max found Lucky sniffing around one of the trash cans in the bathroom. When Max tried to pull him away, Lucky barked and barked. Max realized that Lucky found something, so he reached his arm in there and pulled out a bag of smack with needles and everything. It could have brought him a lot of money if he got it to the right people. Somebody probably stashed it in the can because of the cops, but Lucky found it first.

PELF. Lucky really was lucky, because he found that shit for Max.

PAINT. But Max never did find the right people, and he was getting sicker everyday. It was the winter, and the owner of that shit found Max before he could get rid of it. One morning in January, around five a.m. in Grant

Park, they found Max in the dumpster behind the pool. And Lucky was frozen right there with him. Poor dog.

PELF. I bet it was Lopez.

PAINT. Max was stupid showing that stuff off.

PELF. Yeah, really stupid.

PAINT. Shows you what's what, I guess.

PELF. I know it ain't easy having a dog when you're outdoors, but that little dog was pretty sweet for Max. Gave him a reason to go on for as long as he did.

PAINT. Yeah, but that little fucker also got him killed.

PELF. You can't say that. They did what they could for each other and then shit just happened.

PAINT. The only thing worse than being a homeless man is being a homeless man's dog.

PELF. There.

PAINT. Huh?

PELF. There's some wisdom.

PAINT. That's not wisdom. That's the truth. The guy could barely feed himself and just think what that poor dog had to do to survive. That's some low-ass shit, being a homeless man's dog.

PELF. At least he got attention and someone to take care of him for a little while. They were both pretty happy until they died.

PAINT. Pelf, take the cart.

PELF. What?

PAINT. Take the damn thing to your grocery store. Do something today other than bothering me here.

PELF. I can have the cart?

PAINT. I need to grab a few things out of it first. *(He begins pulling items from the cart.)* Let's see. A lot of this stuff is just shit, plain and simple.*(He holds up a wooden crutch.*) I figured that if I ever hurt myself... well, you know. (*Pulls out a sack of onions.*) I got these last week. I'll cook them up and eat them sometime. (*Roll of toilet paper in one hand, cooking pot in the other.*) Yeah, it's good to scale down. (*Pulls out various items.*) You keep these things for a while, these treasures. Then you wake up one morning and realize that it's all a bunch of shit. You forget why you even kept them in the first place. Don't really need any one thing after a while. There, it's yours now. (*PELF doesn't move.*) Take it. Take it away. Get your fifty dollars.

PELF. I can't. You can't give it to me.

PAINT. It's what you came here for. Take it away.

PELF. No.

PAINT. Take it and go. Or just go away. I want to be by myself now, and that means you can have the damn thing.

PELF. You can't just give it to me. That's not right. I have to take it. I have to steal it from you.

PAINT. What?

PELF. I don't take charity.

PAINT. OK then, steal it.

PELF. No. See, you're giving it to me. You can't give it to me.

PAINT. You're messed up, aren't you?

PELF. I'm not taking this.

PAINT. You can steal Lopez's stuff, but you can't take this?

PELF. Listen. This ain't stealing, OK? This is charity, and I won't take fucking charity, all right? I've got a job that pays money.

PAINT. Bullshit. You think you're gonna make money at a job that forces you to steal from your friends? That's a tripped-out idea of employment.

PELF. Screw it. I'll just knock over some guy that has what I want and thinks he's better than me.

PAINT. Wait a minute. Earlier today you were going to take my cart. You thought I was better than you. But now, you don't want it. You think you're better than me? Take the cart, Fucko.

PELF. Fuck you.

PAINT. What in the hell are you thinking? That you're going to ride away to Wyoming like a cowboy? You don't think Lopez will find you?

PELF. I'm safe here. Lopez won't find me here.

PAINT. The hell he won't. He's got a hundred little shits working for him. Little crack-smoking kids who watch everything that goes on. He has people like you who watch silly old men walk out of the city and into the suburbs. He probably knows you are here right now.

PELF. He can't know.

PAINT. What if he does?

PELF. I take him out.

PAINT. That's funny. You have a tough enough time trying to whoop my shit, and I know that Lopez is a hundred times tougher.

PELF. Well... well... Fuck that.

PAINT. What will you do? Huh? You know that Lopez will find you. It's only a matter of time until he talks to the guy who roughed you up. What's his name? Sweetie?

PELF. But it can't...

PAINT. You see, Pelf, your problem is that you think you've escaped. You think Lopez won't find you. You think Lopez won't care about a little bag of drugs. You're wrong. You're not a man, Pelf. A man doesn't try to escape every time there's trouble. You know what you are?

PELF. What?

PAINT. You're a dog. A dog, Pelf. You're a dog to that grocery store that pays you money to steal from your friends. You're a dog to your drugs. You're a dog to Lopez, and you've always been a dog to me.

PELF. I'm not a dog.

PAINT. You're gonna have to stand up to Lopez, man. Stand up. Upright. Straight-backed. Good. Look me in the eye. In the eye.

PELF. So, what do I do now?

PAINT. Get ready. Stand up to Lopez. Work something out.

PELF. I don't know what to do. Maybe I should just take your cart and go to Safeway, get the fifty dollars and go to Wyoming. I need a car... (*Sound of a car pulling up.*)

PAINT. Shhhh... Wait a minute. Lopez.

PELF. Oh shit. I'm dead. Oh shit, oh shit, oh shit. He looks pissed. What do I do? Hide me.

PAINT. Get in the cart.

(*PELF climbs into the cart talking wildly. PAINT grabs the wad of paper that holds Lopez's tooth and shoves it into PELF's mouth. He then throws a blanket over the cart. LOPEZ enters.*)

LOPEZ. Say what, Paint. What are you doing so far away from town?

PAINT. You know. Just staying away from the police. This is a pretty good spot. It's kind of far from Oldtown.

LOPEZ. Yeah. Oldtown is pretty messed up. Wouldn't want to be there right now. A lot of people are getting pushed around, getting thrown into jail. By the way, have you seen Pelf around?

PAINT. Pelf? No. I thought all of you guys got picked up in the sweep last night.

LOPEZ. No. Not all of us. Pelf got away. Or at least that's what Sweetie told me.

PAINT. Sweetie said that, huh? I guess the cops got him then.

LOPEZ. Sweetie's dead. See, I got picked up by the police, and it seems that somebody stole something important from me, and when I got out of the lockup I had to make sense of what happened. You know a guy can't sit there and be lied to. And man, was Sweetie floating some lies. He said that Pelf took something that was mine and that he got into a fight with him.

PAINT. Wow, Sweetie said Pelf did that?

LOPEZ. It's a shame about Sweetie, but I just hate being lied to. *(He realizes that he has stepped on PELF's jacket.)*

PAINT. Yeah. I know what it's like.

LOPEZ. Are you sure you haven't seen Pelf? Because it's real important that I talk to him. And it would be really bad to have you lying to me about this situation. Seeing what happened to Sweetie and all.

PAINT. You know what, Lopez? Now that I think about it, I have seen Pelf. I wanted to tell you about this as soon as I could, but it's kind of a long story.

LOPEZ. You're in luck, I have some time. Why don't you tell me?

PAINT. Well, you know how messed up Pelf is?

LOPEZ. Yes.

PAINT. And you know about Max and his bull terrier?

LOPEZ. I know about Max.

PAINT. Pelf loves for me to tell him stories. And his favorite is the one about how Max finds his dog and names it Lucky. All of this trouble in Oldtown has really pushed Pelf over the edge. I mean, you know how crazy he was before all of this stuff went down, right?

LOPEZ. Pelf is on the edge of something.

PAINT. Well, all of these problems kind of hit him deeply. And now, I think Pelf has really lost it. You know, when I left Oldtown yesterday, it took me a long time to pull my cart up here. During the trip, I got this feeling that something was following me. I thought I made a quiet getaway, without anybody seeing I had left.

LOPEZ. The lady who sleeps in front of the Buick dealership said you came this way.

PAINT. Yeah, I figured someone must have seen me, but at the time I thought I was alone. Then I saw him. It was Pelf, but he didn't look OK. He scared me at first. He was crawling on his hands and knees, sniffing at things. It was disturbing, because I thought I knew the guy. But you know, everyone on the street has a freak inside of them just waiting to bust out. Well, I finally settled myself here at this bridge, when Pelf springs out at me and starts barking. I think Pelf was so upset with what happened in Oldtown that he changed himself into a dog. But not just any dog, see, he loved that stupid story so much. He thinks he is Max's dog. He thinks he's Lucky. *(PAINT pulls the blanket away to reveal PELF.)*

LOPEZ. Are you fucking with me?

PAINT. No, Lopez, I would not do that. I know how important you are and that it's important for you to talk to Pelf, but, man, I have to tell you, this guy is messed up. Look at this. *(PAINT pets PELF.)* Hey, Lucky! It's OK. It's OK.

LOPEZ. What's that thing in his mouth?

PAINT. Oh, that's just a piece of paper or something. He picks up the weirdest shit. This morning I had to take this dirty tennis ball out of his mouth. I don't know where he picks these things up.

LOPEZ *(takes the paper out of PELF's mouth)*. What is this? There's a tooth inside this. Where did he get this?

PAINT. I don't know where in the world he finds these things. This guy is way fucked up.

LOPEZ. Son of a bitch! This is my tooth. Where in the fuck...

PAINT. Bad dog. Where did you get that? Where did you get that? He doesn't talk at all, Lopez. I try to get him to say stuff, but he won't.

LOPEZ. Shit.

PAINT. I'd better take him to get some food, hope you don't mind.

LOPEZ. Stop. Let me have a look at him. Yeah, his eyes look like he's really out of it. Looks scared too. I would say this man is a dog. C'mere, Lucky.

PELF (*jumps out of the cart*). Woof.

LOPEZ. That's a good dog. C'mere, don't be afraid. Does he do any tricks?

PAINT. Uh... Uh... Yeah. Roll over, Lucky. (*PELF rolls over.*) Uh... Speak, Lucky. (*PELF barks.*)

LOPEZ. Does he fetch?

PAINT. I don't know, but... (*PAINT picks up the tennis ball.*) Here, Lucky. (*PELF runs up to PAINT. PAINT throws the ball, PELF chases after it.*)

LOPEZ. Well, I'll be damned. Look at him go. Come back here, boy! Drop the ball. Good boy. Now here, Lucky. (*LOPEZ pushes the tooth up to his nose.*) Where did you get this? Where did you get this? Huh? (*He kicks PELF in the ribs, PELF yelps and rolls over.*)

PAINT. Lopez, you don't have to...

LOPEZ. Shut up. I've had it with your bullshit. OK, Lucky, (*He pulls a gun and aims it at PELF.*) play dead. (*He searches PELF and finds the bag.*) Whoops, what's this? Guess I shot the wrong dog today.

PAINT. Hold on a sec...

LOPEZ. I said, shut the hell up.

PAINT. You can't shoot him here. People will hear the gunshot and call the police.

LOPEZ. You're right. Gimme that.

PAINT. What? (*LOPEZ rips the scarf from around PAINT's neck and begins strangling PELF.*)

PELF (*struggles against LOPEZ*). PAINT! Paint! Oh God! Oh help...

LOPEZ. Hey! We've got a talker! (*They struggle a moment longer before PELF dies.*) It's never a good day when you have to kill a dog. Well, at least not for the dog. There you go, old man. There's a story for you.

Not like people ever listen to your stories. They're about as full of shit as you are. I gotta say, this one was kind of funny. He thought he was a dog. Shit, I never heard of anything so dumb in my whole life. You didn't save his life, but you did buy him a few extra minutes. Thought he was a dog. I was going to shoot him as soon as I saw him. Damn, that was funny. Well. *(LOPEZ throws the scarf back around PAINT's neck.)* See you back in Oldtown, old man. *(LOPEZ exits. PAINT picks PELF up and places him in the cart. He places the scarf on PELF's chest and wheels the cart offstage. Blackout.)*

END

ADULT AMERICAN MALES

Graham Gordy
University of Central Arkansas

CHARACTERS

WALLACE: 30. Married. Lives and works in Booneville, Ark.
CARL: 30. Married. Wallace's best friend, also lives and works in Booneville.
HOYT: 30. Single. Now lives and works in Fayetteville, Ark.
EDGAR: 30. Married. Now lives and works in Chicago, Ill.

PLACE: A small summer cabin set in the Arkansas Ozarks.

TIME: The present.

NOTE: This play should maintain a level of fast-paced drinking, indulgence, and crudity. The characters' sobriety should diminish more and more with each scene until the end in which there is a certain amount of clarity. There will need to be videotaped clips of years past projected onto the stage to open the play, as segues between scenes, and to close it. These scenes should be of absurd stunts and memorable events which adequately display each of the characters' personalities.

ADULT AMERICAN MALES was first staged by the University of Central Arkansas on October 30, 1997 with the following cast:

Wallace .... DAVID WOOD
Carl .... MARC HOFRICHTER
Hoyt. .... JASON SHOCKLEY
Edgar. .... CHRIS COLLINS

Staged by Dr. Bob Willenbrink

ADULT AMERICAN MALES

SCENE ONE

SETTING: *Hoyt's cabin. The set is a living room and a kitchen with a front entrance L. There is a couch and a rocking chair in the living room, R, and only hard, wooden furniture in the kitchen. There is a door U that leads to a bedroom and bathroom.*

AT RISE: *It's a late Friday afternoon. John Prine's "Yes I Guess They Oughta Name a Drink After You" starts.* WALLACE and CARL are at the sink filling water balloons and sticking them in a cooler. They are talking, laughing, and drinking. Through the front entrance enters HOYT holding EDGAR in a headlock. In EDGAR's hands are a small travel bag and a large basketful of snacks.*

HOYT. Hey, assholes! Look what I found.
WALLACE & CARL. Hey! Eddie! Whooo! *(Howls and grunts are exchanged. Both WALLACE and CARL give EDGAR greeting noogies as HOYT keeps casually holding him in a headlock.)*
EDGAR. Hey, Hoyt. *(He points to the arm around his neck.)*
WALLACE. We didn't think you were gonna make it.
CARL. We thought you got caught up changing diapers or something.

---

* The music suggested throughout this piece is preferred, but director's choice of music may be substituted.

WALLACE. What's in the basket?

HOYT (*mockingly*). Aww. Did you bring us a picnic?

EDGAR. No, Margot just baked some cookies and things. (*By this time the men have grabbed the basket and are rummaging through it. HOYT releases EDGAR's head and goes to meet others. They are opening and consuming a bag of cookies.*) Wait. Let me get the camera. Margot will want to see your reaction to her cookies. (*EDGAR crosses to his bag and gets his video camera, begins filming as they start eating. A pause as the group agrees on their disgust.*)

HOYT (*spitting cookie out*). Oh Jesus, Ed.

CARL. Why do your wife's cookies always taste like beef jerky?

WALLACE. These are... No, these are definitely the worst cookies I've ever had.

HOYT. You caught you a good-looking wife, but she can't cook worth a shit.

EDGAR. OK. She probably won't want to see that at all.

CARL. Are those Cheetos? (*All converge on the basket, pass around the bag. WALLACE sits on the couch, CARL in the rocking chair, while HOYT sits by the kitchen table. There is only silence and crunching. Everyone is staring the same direction out into space.*)

WALLACE. Hell... Another year.

HOYT. We are thirty fucking years old, gentlemen.

WALLACE. Why are you recording this? Are you gonna take this back home and show it to your Yankee kids?

EDGAR. It's just so I can have a record. I've been doing it for ten years. It's all for the reel. So go ahead and talk... like you normally would.

WALLACE (*in a ridiculous, mocking tone*). So... How has your year been, Eddie?

EDGAR. Why do I have to go first?

WALLACE. 'Cause Carl and I see each other every goddamn day, and Hoyt only lives an hour and a half away from us. But nobody ever talks to you till we see you here.

EDGAR. I've been busy. I work a lot. Margot's doing great. She's working a lot more now. Ben's playing T-ball, and Sally's already talking.

HOYT. How old are they now?

CARL. Do we have to talk about our goddamn wives and kids? Why don't you just put on your apron that says "World's Greatest Dad" and we can pull out the fucking pictures. This is just the one time every year that I get away from my wife and kids and can just be...a man...with other men.

HOYT. I'll start. (*Mockingly.*) My dick's so big I could pick up that refrigerator with it.

CARL. Don't be an asshole.

EDGAR. He's got a point, Carl. We're getting old, and we can't just sit around and talk about drinking beer and getting pussy like we used to.

CARL. Why not? (*Moves to the refrigerator, and passes out beers to everyone.*) We've got our normal, pathetic lives the rest of the year. Why can't we just forget all that shit for one weekend?

WALLACE. Probably because we don't consider our lives shit, Carl. That way we don't mind talking about 'em.

HOYT. Now just calm down. I think you boys spend too much time together. You're gonna have to just fight it out once and for all one of these days. (*A long pause. WALLACE and CARL stare at each other.*)

CARL. The usual? (*WALLACE nods and everyone gets up. WALLACE and CARL go to the center of the room. HOYT kicks a small rug out of the way and stands between them. WALLACE and CARL look beastly as they playfully stalk one another. EDGAR begins circling WALLACE and CARL with his camera.*)

HOYT. You gotta pin both shoulders. No biting, no shots below the belt... Hell, you know the rules. (*To WALLACE.*) You ready? (*To CARL.*) You ready? (*WALLACE slaps CARL around a bit to get him angry. CARL charges WALLACE and they struggle for a while. The fight is long, funny and ridiculous, utilizing a large portion of the set. The stage is silent except for their grunting. WALLACE finally pins CARL to win. WALLACE parades around victoriously, moons the camera, etc. CARL is on the ground sitting up, catching his breath as EDGAR approaches him with the camera. HOYT begins to act as a television commentator.*) Well, Carl, you didn't give him much of a fight at all out there. As a matter of fact, it was a weak effort and we, along with all our viewers at home, pretty much consider you a big pussy now.

CARL. Get that out of my face. (*CARL gets up and moves to the kitchen. He finishes off his beer and gets another one for WALLACE and himself.*)

EDGAR. You boys will never change.

WALLACE. You act like that's a bad thing.

EDGAR. It's not a bad thing. That's why we're here. You guys come up here to rebel.

CARL. Rebel? Rebel against what?

WALLACE. Don't exclude yourself there, Dickbreath.

EDGAR. Women. Your jobs. Take your pick. You come up here to say "fuck it" to feminism or your wives or whatever else is frustrating you.

WALLACE. Feminism? What the hell are you talking about? Feminism?

EDGAR. This is what it's about. The modern American man getting away from having to be a sensitive guy or caring husband and telling people "fuck you" when you feel like it. It's kinda like a support group. We got each other.

CARL. Support group. I like that.

WALLACE. Support group? Oh, kiss ass.

HOYT. If you boys are done shaking your dicks at each other, maybe we can get a little fishing in before we run out of daylight.

EDGAR. He's right, boys. *(Loudly.)* We came here to fish. *(Everyone yells and howls in agreement. All start grabbing equipment and heading for the door. WALLACE grabs his cooler on the way out. The stage goes to black. John Prine's "Donald & Lydia" starts.)*

SCENE TWO

AT RISE: *EDGAR storms in with his hair dripping wet. HOYT is behind him carrying several fish and a six-pack holder with one beer in it. It's still light outside.*

EDGAR. How old are they, Hoyt? How fucking old are they? Water balloons? *(EDGAR finds a towel and starts drying off. HOYT goes to the kitchen, puts on an apron and starts scaling and cleaning the fish.)*

HOYT. At least he didn't throw you in the river like last year.

EDGAR (*pause*). I can handle this. I can do this, Hoyt. You know why? Because I've got him. No matter what he says or does to me, no matter how many times he gets the best of me, I've still (*Yells.*) fucked his wife! ...And before him. It's beautiful.

HOYT (*looking towards the door*). Keep your voice down!

EDGAR. They can't hear us. They're still down there trying to see who can make the loudest fart noise with their armpits. (*Pause.*) I'd just love to tell him sometimes.

HOYT. Now don't get stupid, 'cause I'm part of this too.

EDGAR. But wouldn't you love it, Hoyt? Wouldn't you love to see the poor bastard's face when we told him that we'd both fucked his (*Makes quotation marks with his hands.*) "virgin bride" before they'd even gone out.

HOYT (*lost in thought*). Yeah.

WALLACE (*in the distance, as he and CARL approach*). So he says, "Hey, Bob, guess who I'm fuckin'?"

(*EDGAR goes to the sink and washes his hands, then begins to clean around the kitchen. WALLACE and CARL enter laughing. CARL is carrying WALLACE's cooler while WALLACE has a water balloon in each hand.*)

WALLACE (*gestures as if he's going to throw one at EDGAR*). What's wrong, Ed? I'm not gonna hit you with one of these.

EDGAR. Grow up, Wallace.

WALLACE. I think he's pissed at me. Carl, do you think he's pissed at me?

CARL. He seems pissed.

WALLACE (crossing to EDGAR). I'm sorry, Ed. Once again we've gotten off to a bad start and I'm...I'm just sick about it. (On his knees. Begins feigning sadness, as if a confessing televangelist.) Carl knows how upset I get if I think I've (Mockingly.) hurt somebody's feelings.

CARL (crossing to repent). We're all sinners here, Wallace. Like the time we broke into the high school and put Quik-Crete in all the toilets.

WALLACE (mockingly). But you didn't do that with us, did you, Ed? (Seriously.) What about the time at the county fair when Jimmy Wayne Jarret left the windows down and we poured two forty-pound bags of cow shit into his truck?

CARL. Now he deserved that, he was a son of a bitch.

WALLACE. Or the time when we were out at the Supper Club and Hoyt about got his ass whooped by that great, big ol' Samoan bitch. (Everyone sighs with laughter. A long pause. EDGAR sits by CARL.) I gotta piss. (WALLACE stands up and starts unbuttoning his pants as he walks outside.)

CARL (to EDGAR). See that? He always does that shit. He just starts whipping it out before he even gets to the bathroom. There oughta be a law against that. Is he in that much of a hurry? Can he not wait till he gets there with the door closed? He even does it in public bathrooms. He'll just pull his cock out and start shopping for a stall.

EDGAR. What can I say, Carl? He's an insensitive asshole.

CARL. He's not so bad.

EDGAR. Yeah he is. He's like a bull in a China shop...
but he's not as smart. He's like a kid too... Like Dennis
the Menace. He's this snot-nose little prick who never
learns his lessons. He just keeps doing the same shit
over and over again. *(CARL looks confused.)* You remember.

CARL. You mean from Andy Griffith?

EDGAR. No, dumbass!

(WALLACE comes back in.)

WALLACE. What are y'all jabbering about?

EDGAR. You... Being a man... Being a big, hulking
brute of a man. Being a big fucking, horse-riding, deer-
hunting, beer-drinking man.

WALLACE. What's in your ass, Ed? What's this all about?

EDGAR. Just trying to figure out why I'm here, why I
come here year after year.

HOYT. Same as us, Ed. You need to get away.

WALLACE. He's just making excuses.

EDGAR. Excuses?

WALLACE. You keep talking about being a man, and
how we're all assholes because of what we do. I don't
think you know what a real man is, 'cause everybody's
always considered you a big pussy.

EDGAR. Why don't you tell me what a real man is? *(Pause.)*

WALLACE. We all played in the state finals, you
watched.

EDGAR. High school football? You're saying that I'm not
a real man because I didn't play high school football?

WALLACE. You can't even change the oil in your car. Every summer we all bailed hay in Waldron. You worked in your dad's furniture store.

EDGAR. Oh, come on. If you could've worked in air conditioning, you would've.

WALLACE. You get out of the shower to take a piss, don't ya.

EDGAR *(gets up and approaches WALLACE).* What else, Wallace? What else? I could never drink as much beer as you. I never fucked as many women as you... But I'll tell you one thing I did, I left this goddamned state. I didn't stay where it was easy, where it was comfortable. I went to college. I didn't live with my goddamn parents till I was twenty-three. *(Searching now, almost to himself.)* I'm a man. I pay my house payment each month... I'm a good dad...

CARL. Are we over this shit now? You think you ladies can get along long enough not to kill each other by Sunday? All right. *(To HOYT.)* Get your ass back in the kitchen, Hop Sing. Now, in order to add a little levity to the situation, I suggest we play a little game of Fantasyfuck. You boys know the rules. Wallace, why don't you go first? *(EDGAR grabs his camera and begins recording again.)*

WALLACE. Definitely Alice's tits. Those things still amaze me.

EDGAR. You can't use your wife.

WALLACE. She graduated with us.

EDGAR. If you use your wife, you might as well be able to use anybody. No, no. Start over.

WALLACE. Ashley Meisner's tits.

HOYT. I regret that. I never saw those.

CARL. Oh, she'd show 'em to ya. All you had to do was ask. You couldn't be an asshole about it or nothing. She wasn't a whore. But if you walked up and said, "Hey, I really like your breasts," or something nice like that, she'd lift up her shirt.

WALLACE. Are you done? *(Slowly, as if visualizing every choice.)* Tracy Ratcliff's ass, Bonnie Smoat's face. And Nancy Jessup's legs.

CARL. Boner time. That would be nice. All right, Ed, your turn.

EDGAR. Laura Davis' eyes.

CARL. What? Eyes? No, no. This game is called Fantasy-fuck. We're talking strictly physical stimulation here.

EDGAR. Eyes are stimulating to me.

CARL. OK. You don't get a turn. *(Yelling to the kitchen.)* Hoyt, let's have yours.

HOYT *(still working on fish)*. Meisner's tits. Who'd you say for ass, Wal?

WALLACE. Tracy Ratcliff.

HOYT. I'll go for that. And Lois Smeltzer's legs.

CARL. What about face?

HOYT. I don't care much for faces.

EDGAR. Your turn, Carl.

CARL. Alice's tits.

WALLACE. What?

CARL. I can use her tits.

WALLACE. That's my wife. If I can't use her, you can't.

CARL. She's got a great set, Wal.

EDGAR. He's right, she does have a great set.

CARL. Stacy Dowdy's legs, Pridmore's ass, and ... Alice's face.

WALLACE. You want to fuck my wife, don't you?

CARL. She's a pretty woman, Wal.

EDGAR *(mockingly)*. It's just a game, Wally.

WALLACE *(to CARL)*. You're an asshole.

CARL. Lighten up, Wallace. You got her. *(Laughing.)* She hardly ever even spends the night anymore.

WALLACE. That's it. Let's go.

(WALLACE goes to the kitchen table. CARL meets him at the table. They sit across from each other. EDGAR crosses with them to record the action. HOYT, in apron, comes to meet them.)

HOYT. OK. This is a one-time deal. *(WALLACE and CARL clasp right hands. HOYT grabs their hands.)* Ready... Set... Go. *(WALLACE and CARL strain with each other for a while. The room is silent except for their grunting. WALLACE finally pins CARL's arm and gets up triumphantly, humming the "Rocky" theme. The stage fades to black. John Prine's "Come Back to Us Barbara Lewis Hare Krishna Beauregard" starts.)*

SCENE THREE

AT RISE: *It's now after dinner. It's gotten dark outside. The mood is lighter, and the men are drunker. HOYT, CARL, and EDGAR are sitting around the dinner table organizing poker chips and putting on dealer's visors. WALLACE enters from the L door buckling his belt.*

WALLACE. What is it about pissing outside? I love it. You can't get a woman to piss outside. *(Pulls out a deck of playing cards, sets them on the table, and sits. HOYT shuffles and begins dealing.)* I just realized it's been ten years. This is our tenth year to do this.

HOYT. You boys don't look the same. I'm glad I'm not as ugly as y'all. What the hell are these?

WALLACE. Nudie cards. You like 'em?

EDGAR. I'm in love with my hand.

WALLACE. That's not the first time.

CARL. Who hasn't anted?

WALLACE. Deuces and jacks and the man with the ax are wild, aces high, and low Chicago.

EDGAR. You can't call it now. *(HOYT is looking at the wrong side of the cards.)*

WALLACE. Look alive there, Hoyt. I can see your cards. How often do you come over here, Hoyt? *(They continue the card game throughout the conversation. WALLACE gets up to get another beer and notices EDGAR's camera unattended. As they are talking, WALLACE takes the camera and begins filming down his pants, flipping-off the camera, etc.)*

HOYT. About every weekend in the summer. Less when it's cold.

CARL. Boy, you got the life. You spend the week with all these women and your weekends here.

HOYT. It's not exactly like that.

CARL *(referring to cards)*. Give me two. You were always one for the ladies. Like that time you nailed Mandy Cartwright before you even knew her name.

EDGAR. What was the story with that anyway?

HOYT. OK. OK. It was our junior year, and she had just moved into town. We were at a party... It was at your house, Ed. That one where we really fucked up your house.

EDGAR. Which one was that?

HOYT. It was the one where they threw your trampoline into the pool, and Shug Davis fell off your gazebo and broke his arm. *(Sounds of agreed recollection from everyone.)* So, Wallace introduced us, and fifteen minutes later I had her in your parent's bathroom with her pants to her knees.

EDGAR. Thanks for at least not fucking her in my parents bed.

HOYT. There was already somebody in there. *(WALLACE raises his hand to take credit for that, then takes his seat again.)*

CARL. Did y'all ever go out after that?

HOYT. No, I didn't talk to her much after that.

WALLACE. Give me one.

HOYT. How many do you want, Ed? *(A long pause as EDGAR shuffles and reshuffles his cards.)*

EDGAR. Five. I want five.

WALLACE. You can't have five.

CARL *(to HOYT)*. Just give him five.

WALLACE. Why don't you make yourself useful and go get me a beer? *(CARL immediately gets up and crosses to the cooler.)*

EDGAR. Now, what's a straight again? *(WALLACE grabs EDGAR's cards out of his hand and tosses them down.)*

CARL *(checking the refrigerator now)*. Who drank the last beer?

WALLACE. The last beer? What do you mean the last beer?

CARL. There's no more beer in here. Didn't anybody bring some more?

WALLACE. You're kidding me. You mean I'm the only one who brought beer?

EDGAR. I just figured we'd get some tomorrow.

CARL. Is there anything else that's here? You bring any of your homegrown, Hoyt?

HOYT. No. *(Searching the cabinets.)* I got a bottle of vermouth and some Margarita mix, but it's non-alcoholic.

WALLACE. Vermouth? What are you doing with Vermouth?

HOYT. It was for a party or something.

WALLACE. All right. Never mind. The fact is that we need beer. Where's the nearest wet county?

CARL. Is Harrison wet?

HOYT. No. Carroll county's the closest, but Baxter is probably easier to get to. But, first of all, by the time you leave you'd be lucky to find anything open, and second, you're drunk.

WALLACE. Good. Then we're off to Baxter. Carl, you coming with me?

CARL. Yep.

EDGAR. We don't need anymore beer tonight. I'll drive there first thing in the morning.

WALLACE. Boys, the night is still young, and I'm not even half in the bag.

HOYT. Let 'em go, Ed.

EDGAR. Jesus... OK, but don't get arrested, don't get in any fights, and don't steal anything.

WALLACE. Y'all play some Scrabble or jackoff or something. We'll be back before you know it. *(He and CARL head for the door with their visors still on.)* Later on, assholes. *(They exit.)*

EDGAR. Fuck-ups.

HOYT. You oughta be used to it by now.

EDGAR. They do something like this every year.

HOYT. Yep. *(Pours a glass of vermouth and motions to EDGAR as an offer. EDGAR declines and takes a seat in rocking chair. HOYT moves to the living room.)*

EDGAR. You'd think they'd grow out of it.

HOYT. If I spent that much time with Wallace, I'd hafta kill him. They spend more time with each other than they do with their wives.

EDGAR. I guess they like each other more than they do their wives.

HOYT. Yeah, I guess. Things in Booneville don't seem to change much. Everybody lives pretty much day to day.

EDGAR. I think Carl would be all right if he'd just get out of Wallace's goddamn shadow. But Wallace needs...

HOYT. Wallace needs an ass-whoopin'.

EDGAR. He always has. Of course, you know that better than me. You see him all the time.

HOYT. Not really.

EDGAR. No?

HOYT. I see his wife every now and then.

EDGAR. What?

HOYT. Not every now and then, just once really.

EDGAR. You mean like...? *(A long pause as HOYT crosses uncomfortably DL.)*

HOYT. I got something to tell ya, Ed. And I can't really laugh about it 'cause I'm probably goin' to hell for doing it. Anyway, something happened a few weeks ago, and I'm not proud of myself for it, and I don't know what to do.

EDGAR. What the hell was it, Hoyt?

HOYT. I was at home one night and I get this call. It's from Alice, and she's at this bar just a few blocks from my house. Well, Alice and I don't really keep in touch that much so I'm wondering what it's all about. She says she's in town for the night, and she's got some conference, right? So then she says something about old times. Bingo. I know what it's about. So there I am in my living room debating in my head if I should go meet her at this bar. I know what's gonna happen if I go, but if I don't... I mean Alice is...

EDGAR. Alice is... Yeah, I know.

HOYT. So, long story short, I go. And we come back to my place, and she's telling me about her and Wallace, and how she needs to do something crazy. So... we did it.

EDGAR. Holy shit, Hoyt.

HOYT. Yeah, I know. I feel like shit for it. I made up all these reasons in my head about why it was OK, but they haven't really held up. As much as I want to get back at Wallace, fucking his wife is a whole different ball game. Before they got together... that's one thing. I could just hold that over his head, but this, this was my friend's wife.

EDGAR. I don't know what to say, Hoyt. *(Pause.)* How was it?

HOYT. Great. Hell, she was an animal. She was never like that in high school.

EDGAR. What are you gonna do? How'd you leave it?

HOYT. What can I do?

EDGAR. Has she done stuff like that before?

HOYT. I don't think so... Maybe. The problem is that it may become more of a normal thing. She comes to Fayetteville a lot, and I'm afraid she expects to do it again.

EDGAR. You can't do that again, Hoyt.

HOYT. I know. Wallace is my friend. He's an asshole, but he's still my friend.

EDGAR. So, what are you gonna tell her?

HOYT. I don't know.

EDGAR. It's not gonna be easy to say no.

HOYT. I know.

EDGAR *(pause)*. And Wallace doesn't have a clue?

HOYT. About us? No.

EDGAR. Damn, Hoyt.

HOYT. It's bugging the hell out of me. I can hardly stand to be in the same room with the son of a bitch.

EDGAR. Don't do anything stupid. Keep your mouth shut. Wallace would kill us all if he found out.

HOYT. Yeah. *(EDGAR stares at HOYT as he is absorbed in his own thought.)*

EDGAR. It'll probably be a while before they get back.

HOYT. God knows where they'll end up.

EDGAR & HOYT. Idiots. *(John Prine's "Spanish Pipedream" starts. The lights fade to black.)*

SCENE FOUR

AT RISE: *The set is the same. HOYT is asleep and the only one on stage. WALLACE and CARL enter through the L door carrying a stop sign, with post, that has obviously been pulled out of the ground, and a twelve-pack of beer. Both men are noticeably drunker.*

WALLACE. Shhh!

(They lightly set down the sign and put some beer in the refrigerator. WALLACE goes in the other room and comes back with a tube of toothpaste. He squeezes the toothpaste on HOYT's forehead while CARL goes to the kitchen and gets a cookie out of EDGAR's basket. CARL smears the toothpaste around and sticks the cookie to his forehead. EDGAR enters from the U door in pajamas, a stick of deodorant in his hand.)

EDGAR. What the hell are you doing?

WALLACE & CARL. Shhh! *(HOYT begins to wake up.)*

HOYT. What the...? Y'all are assholes! *(Gets up and walks to the bathroom.)* I'm gonna get you fuckers for this.

EDGAR *(pointing to the stop sign)*. What the hell is this? *(WALLACE and CARL begin to laugh.)*

CARL. Nothing.

WALLACE. Just something we picked up on the way back.

EDGAR. Somebody could have a wreck.

WALLACE *(mockingly)*. Somebody could have a wreck.

EDGAR. Did you yank it out of the ground?

WALLACE. Yeah, it took the both of us.

(HOYT comes back in, wiping off his face with a towel.)

CARL. It was heavy as shit.

HOYT *(pointing to the sign)*. What is this shit?

WALLACE. Nearest I can figure it's a stop sign, Hoyt.

HOYT. Yeah. What's it doing here?

CARL. We tried to take it off the post, but I didn't have a ratchet in the truck.

HOYT. Just take the son of a bitch with you when you leave. Did you actually find any beer?

WALLACE. Yeah. I thought we were on our way to Mountain Home, but we ended up at a place called Big Flat... There was a store there... Open all night. *(EDGAR starts putting on the deodorant.)* What the hell are you doing?

EDGAR. Putting on deodorant.

CARL. You're going to bed!

EDGAR. I don't wanna stink before I go to bed.

CARL. Jesus.

WALLACE. What've you jerkoffs been doing since we left?

EDGAR. Just talking.

WALLACE. Carl, get these boys a beer. *(CARL crosses to the refrigerator.)*

EDGAR. No need, Carl. I'm done drinking for the night.

HOYT. I'll take one.

WALLACE. Done drinking? *(Crosses to EDGAR and points at him.)* We're never done drinking, boy, not when we're here.

EDGAR. Get outta my face, Douchebag.

WALLACE. Oooo. Somebody's testy. Did we interrupt something boys? You want we should leave you alone? If y'all were about to start chugging some cock we can go outside or something.

EDGAR. Fuck off, Wallace. *(CARL hands HOYT and EDGAR beers. EDGAR hesitates, then finally accepts. WALLACE stands ominously next to him, guzzles his beer, and belches in EDGAR's face. EDGAR takes a drink as WALLACE stares at him.)* What?

WALLACE. Peer pressure's a bitch, ain't it?

EDGAR. Just 'cause your a fucking drunk most of the time doesn't mean we all are.

WALLACE. What's that, Ed?

EDGAR. You heard me... Drunk. You're a drunk. Two counties over in the middle of the night for beer?

WALLACE. I don't drink like this all the time. This is us. This is what we do.

EDGAR. No, this is what *you* do. You just come up here to get somebody else to do it with you.

WALLACE. Fuck you, Ed. You don't even know me. You don't even see me except when we're here. How would you know how I am? (*EDGAR looks at HOYT to back him up. Silence.*)

CARL. We're all different when we're here, Ed. We aren't really like this. This is where we can drink like this, and we can be vulgar as all hell. This is where it's allowed.

EDGAR (*begins picking up beer cans, cleaning*). I just see the same shit, year after year.

WALLACE. Pardon me, Your Highness. Yeah, we come up here to drink and to say fuck and shit. And we know why we're up here. Get off your high horse, Ed. You think you're the only one that knows? We do this shit 'cause it's like high school again. Some of us like high school.

EDGAR. I *liked* high school. I like coming up here...

WALLACE (*crossing to him*). Then enjoy yourself, for Chrissake. If you spend all your time bellyaching then what fun are you having? Quit being the goddamn dad! (*Knocks empty cans out of EDGAR's hands.*)

EDGAR. Somebody has to. If I don't do it, who will?

HOYT. Will you two quit? Jesus. I'll tell you what I'm tired of. None of y'all can go ten minutes without getting in an argument. We're too old for this shit.

CARL. You're never too old to argue, Hoyt.

HOYT. I'm not talking about that. I'm talking about coming up here. It seems like we can't even get along for a weekend anymore.

WALLACE. Nothing's changed, Hoyt. It's always been like this. Seems to me like you're just getting soft.

HOYT. Well, maybe I just don't give a shit anymore.

CARL. You live alone. You get to act like a kid all the time. The rest of us need a little time away.

HOYT. What? Susan took away your playroom?

CARL. Real funny, Assbreath.

WALLACE. That's not the only thing she took away.

EDGAR. Ooh. (*Gets his camera and begins recording.*)

CARL. Shut up, Wallace.

EDGAR. What's wrong, Carl? Is Susan withholding the big V from you these days?

CARL (*to EDGAR*). Turn that fucking thing off. It was more of a mutual decision.

WALLACE. Yeah, she decided to kick your ass out of the bedroom, and you decided to go.

CARL. Wallace.

WALLACE. Oh, come on, Carl. I'm just fucking with you. So, you guys are having some problems. Everybody has problems.

CARL (*crossing to WALLACE and getting in his face*). Well, ours ain't even worth talking about so shut the fuck up.

WALLACE. I think this lack of nookie is getting to you, boy. I got a few phone numbers if you wanna fix that.

CARL. I don't need your whores, Wallace. We'll be fine. We'll be just fine.

WALLACE (*spills beer all over his shirt*). Fuck.

HOYT. You need a bib there, Swillpot?

WALLACE. I need a steak. Are we cooking steaks tomorrow?

EDGAR. Yeah, we're cooking steaks.

WALLACE. I love steak. I could eat steak every night.

CARL. It'd kill you.

WALLACE. My ass. Do you believe that? My ass. Steak ain't any worse for you than anything else. You eat chicken every night and you'll die just as quick. Salmonella and all that... Little fuckers are evil.

CARL. I thought you got Salmonella from fish.

WALLACE. It'll all kill you. (*EDGAR turns off his camera, looks at his watch and starts to move toward the bedroom.*)

EDGAR. It's almost three a.m., boys. I think I'm gonna hit the rack.

HOYT. Come on, Ed. Stay up with us. You don't have to get up for anything in the morning.

WALLACE. You know we're gonna fuck with you if you go to sleep, Ed. Besides, it's time to play a drinking game.

EDGAR. Christ, Wallace. Let's just save that for tomorrow night.

WALLACE. Where's a shot glass, Hoyt? (*WALLACE begins rummaging through the cabinets. HOYT brings a small juice glass to the kitchen table. CARL seats himself on one side of the table while HOYT gets another beer. EDGAR is still by the bedroom door.*) We'll use this. Who's got a quarter? Who's got a quarter?!

CARL. I got a quarter. *(Hands WALLACE the quarter. WALLACE bounces it off the table into the glass, points at EDGAR.)*

WALLACE. Drink, Bitch. *(Fade to black. John Prine's "Please Don't Bury Me" starts.)*

SCENE FIVE

AT RISE: *When the lights come up EDGAR is seated alone at the kitchen table. WALLACE is asleep on the couch and CARL is throwing up into the kitchen sink. HOYT is asleep in the rocking chair. EDGAR is sipping a beer and looking through a photo album.*

EDGAR *(to CARL).* ... And that was the Christmas party when Wallace passed out and we wrapped him in Christmas lights. *(To himself.)* How did he always end up naked? And this was the night... *(CARL slowly comes back to the table and takes drinks out of old beers to get the taste out of his mouth. EDGAR continues to laugh to himself as he looks through the pictures.)*

CARL. Shut up, Ed! I need silence. *(Pause.)* Now, Hoyt... is a lucky son of a bitch. He can do whatever he wants.

EDGAR. You would really like to live like him?

CARL. Hell yeah! You don't know what I'd do to live alone again.

EDGAR. I couldn't do it.

CARL. Nobody to tell you what to do... Nobody in your way...

EDGAR. Yeah, but wouldn't you get lonely. There's something nice about coming home to a house full of people. What Hoyt's got is nice for a while, but he's too old to be living like that.

CARL. I'd take it any day. Being a family man for the last five years is enough to last me a lifetime.

EDGAR. I know that you and Susan hadn't really planned on getting hitched, but for some reason I thought it'd work out all right.

CARL. It was one of those damned if you do, damned if you don't, you know? *(They pause and look at WALLACE.)*

EDGAR. You think we oughta do something cruel to that son of a bitch?

CARL. No. I know he's an asshole, but...I don't know. If you spent more time with him you'd probably understand why. He's been going through some tough times lately.

EDGAR. What's going on?

CARL *(looks to make sure he's asleep)*. Look, if he knew I was telling you this he'd kill me, so this is between me and you. *(Pause.)* He can't have kids. Him and Susan have been trying for like three years now, and they just found out that his...fish don't swim. I don't think they're gonna be together too much longer. Poor bastard, he's blind to it. But Alice wanted kids three or four years ago. A woman gets impatient over that kind of thing.

EDGAR. They can't adopt?

CARL. You know how Alice is, she wants to do it all... Experience it. Plus, Wallace is no better to her than he is to us. He runs around on her. He gets with all these women to prove that he's still a man. A woman like Alice ain't gonna stick around.

EDGAR. I feel kinda sorry for him now. I just thought they didn't want to have any kids.

CARL. Nope.

EDGAR. That's gotta be tough. *(A pause as EDGAR and CARL look over at him. WALLACE's eyes pop open.)*

WALLACE. What are you doing?

CARL. Nothing.

WALLACE. Were y'all talking about me?

EDGAR. No. We were just talking about ... us and stuff.

WALLACE. What time is it?

EDGAR. About four. You didn't last long in that game.

WALLACE. I gotta piss. *(Gets up, starts unbuckling his belt, and walks outside.)*

CARL. You think he heard us?

EDGAR. No way.

CARL. I'm serious. Don't say a word.

EDGAR. Relax. I'm not gonna say anything, Little Buddy.

CARL. Little Buddy?

EDGAR. That's what you two remind me of, the Skipper and Gilligan. You're Gilligan.

CARL. From *Sanford and Son*?

EDGAR. Where did you grow up?

(WALLACE comes from outside zipping up his pants and sits down at the table.)

WALLACE. How's memory lane this year, Carl?

EDGAR. What do you think about Hoyt's situation? Would you want to live like him?

WALLACE. What do you mean?

EDGAR. You know, living alone... Being free.

WALLACE. I used to. Hell, I guess I still do. If I had to do it over again and all that. I don't know though. Sometimes I come home and Alice isn't there. It gets to feeling pretty lonely. I don't know if I could stand coming home to nothing every night. *(Awkward silence.)* I'm hungry. You think if we woke Hoyt up he'd fix us something to eat? I want some eggs.

EDGAR. Not now, they're for breakfast.

WALLACE. What time do you think it is?

EDGAR. I can't eat now. We'll be ready for lunch at ten a.m.

WALLACE. Do you have a schedule for everything?

EDGAR. I just know my stomach.

CARL *(crosses to HOYT and starts nudging him, yelling).* Hoyt... Wake up, it's time for breakfast.

HOYT. What time is it? It's still dark outside.

CARL. We want eggs. We want eggs! *(Crosses back to the table. HOYT gets up and goes to the kitchen, starts preparing breakfast.)*

HOYT. What do I look like? Martha fucking Stewart? Why doesn't anybody ever cook for me?

WALLACE. 'Cause you're used to it.

HOYT. When are you dickheads gonna learn to cook for yourselves? What's gonna happen if one of you gets a divorce?

EDGAR. We'll have to move in with you.

WALLACE. I guess it's not all good living by yourself. You get lonely, Hoyt?

HOYT. What d'ya mean?

WALLACE. I mean up there in Fayetteville, living alone and all that. Are you happy?

HOYT. Yeah, I guess. You mean because I'm not married?

WALLACE. Yeah.

HOYT. I don't know how to react to that, Wal. Of course I get lonely sometimes, but that's nothing that a wife could keep me from. You get lonely too...I bet, just as much as me, and you got all those people around you. The difference is when I get lonely I can just ask somebody over for a while, but when you get lonely you're stuck with who you got.

CARL *(almost whispering)*. Stuck with who we got... *(John Prine's "Paradise" starts. The stage goes to black.)*

SCENE SIX

AT RISE: *The lights come; up all four men, seated around the kitchen table. They have finished their breakfast. A bit of sunlight can be seen through the windows.*

WALLACE. ...But I think Carl takes the cake for dumbass moves when he thought he could jump Sludge Creek in his truck.

HOYT. You filled up the whole floorboard with water, didn't you? *(Everyone laughs except for CARL.)*

CARL. I was drunk.

WALLACE. You weren't drunk. You just don't wanna admit that it was a dumbass thing to do.

CARL. You're no stranger to dumbass moves. How 'bout the time you picked up that girl that turned out to be your boss' nineteen-year-old daughter?

HOYT. What?

WALLACE. Thanks, Carl.

HOYT. You screwed your boss' daughter?

CARL. He didn't screw her...

WALLACE. I found out her last name before anything happened.

EDGAR. Did he ever find out?

WALLACE. She. My boss is a she, and no, she didn't.

EDGAR. I know this is none of my business, but you seem to fuck around a lot.

WALLACE. Not a lot. Just when the situation arises.

EDGAR. I don't get it. I don't see how you get all these women.

WALLACE. Hell, Ed. I'm irresistible.

EDGAR. I mean, do you work with these women?

WALLACE. No. They're always around if you're looking. Are you asking me why I mess around?

EDGAR. No, I know why you mess around.

WALLACE. Really? What the fuck would you know about it?

EDGAR. You're trying to get back at 'em. You can't deal with 'em in any capacity anymore. At home, they're telling you what to do and what not to do. At work, they've got all sorts of new power, so you've got all new reasons to hate 'em. But you can't hate 'em, not openly at least.

WALLACE. I don't hate women.

EDGAR. Oh, yeah you do. You just don't know how to deal with it. But you can still fuck 'em, can't you, Wallace?

WALLACE. I guess things just aren't as perfect for me and Alice as they are for you and what's-her-name.

You act like I'm the only one who's ever done it before. Some people just need to. Carl should. His wife is certainly taking her liberties.

CARL. Goddammit, Wallace. Don't start talking about things you don't know nothing about. *(EDGAR gets his camera and begins recording.)*

WALLACE. Wise up, Carl. Everybody knows.

CARL. Well, everybody can't have a wife that'll put up with all the shit that Alice puts up with. Not everybody's got a wife that'll let her husband cheat on her. *(He stands.)*

WALLACE. What's this fucking obsession with my wife? Who's your friend here?

CARL. I'm your friend, and as your friend I'm telling you that you're a fucking dickhead. You just don't deserve her.

WALLACE. Just 'cause your wife's gotten all fatty boom-balatty in the last few years doesn't mean that you need to start getting your bone up over mine.

CARL. That's it. Fuck you, Wallace. *(He crosses to the center of the living room ready to fight. WALLACE crosses to him arrogantly and begins to push and slap at him playfully.)*

WALLACE *(laughing)*. How is it fucking her big, fat ass? Huh? Huh, Carl? *(Both men are in a wrestling stance and circling around the room. There is a much more serious air to the situation in CARL. EDGAR puts his camera down.)*

EDGAR. Jesus. Lay off, Wal.

WALLACE. I'm just playing with him. *(CARL charges WALLACE and they struggle with each other for a long while. There is a ferocity that wasn't there before. They grapple as the fight grows more and more fierce. WAL-LACE is at first surprised by CARL's aggression, but soon matches it. The stage is silent except for their grunting. WALLACE eventually pins CARL's shoulders to the ground. He stands to walk away as CARL pushes him and spins him around. It looks as though CARL is going to attack him again when he realizes that he is powerless. WALLACE tackles CARL and pins him again so there will be no question who the winner is. EDGAR runs up and tries to separate them.)*

EDGAR. Stop! Stop! *(WALLACE pushes EDGAR away and gets off of CARL angrily, confused about what has happened.)*

WALLACE. What's this all about, Carl?

CARL. Don't you see? You won.

WALLACE. Of course I won. I always win.

CARL. Exactly. You always win, and I'm tired of it. Every sport, every argument, every fight. You win, Wallace. And you got the girl too.

WALLACE. Who?

CARL. Alice, you blind motherfucker! Your wife, Alice.

WALLACE. Y'all never even went out.

CARL. I was her best friend since sixth grade.

WALLACE. What about Susan?

CARL. What about Susan? Do you think I'm happy with Susan?

WALLACE. Then why'd you marry her?

CARL. 'Cause I couldn't have Alice! You don't give a shit about her. She was always just there for you. You don't spend any time with her. I don't even care anymore. I don't even want her. But you don't deserve her. It's not even about her anymore. You won! That's what it's about. Alice and I are inseparable, then you move into town and I don't see her anymore. I set you up. I got you together. What a stupid fucker I was. How do you thank me? You treat her like shit, you treat me like shit...

WALLACE. Why didn't you tell me about this?

CARL. I don't know. I thought you were happy. I thought you were gonna be happy. If I'd known how shitty it was gonna turn out, I would've fought for her.

WALLACE. What do you mean shitty?

CARL. Oh, come on. You haven't been happy since high school. You cheat on her.

WALLACE. It's no different from you and Susan.

CARL. Me and Susan never had a chance. We stay together to piss each other off. But you and Alice... Homecoming Queen and football stud. Y'all were supposed to be all right. You think she doesn't know about you? She doesn't give a shit about you anymore. You've made her hate you. What pisses me off is that she's fucked everybody in this room except me.

WALLACE. What?

CARL *(enjoying it)*. Yeah, I guess you didn't know that. That's right. Your best buddies here plugged your little lovely before you did.

WALLACE. What are you talking about?

CARL. They fucked her... Fuuuucked! *(Pause.)*

WALLACE *(sadly)*. Is that true, guys?

EDGAR. Look, Wallace. It was nothing.

WALLACE. You're kidding me. Both of you? *(Silence as WALLACE stares into their faces.)* When did this happen?

EDGAR. It doesn't matter. It was before you were even in the picture.

WALLACE. My ass it doesn't matter. *(Moves closer to them.)* That's my wife.

EDGAR. Now just calm down, Wallace.

WALLACE. Calm down? This is my wife. Now you're telling me that not only did she fuck two people...

HOYT. You weren't even married then.

WALLACE *(gradually building to anger)*. But you're telling me that my *girlfriend* not only fucked two other people, but that those people were two of my best friends? Fuck you... Fuck her!

CARL. As I remember it, you weren't exactly innocent in all this yourself. You had your share of flings.

WALLACE. Fuck you, Carl. I told Alice about everything I'd done. And wipe that grin off your face. She swore to me she'd never fucked anybody. Why didn't you tell me? *(He gets in EDGAR's face.)* Ed? When did this happen?

EDGAR. It was before you went out.

WALLACE. When? Hoyt? Who was first? Who fucked her first?

EDGAR. Why are you doing this, Wallace?

WALLACE. Because my wife's a whore and I'm just finding out about it.

CARL. You're wife's not a whore. You're the whore.

WALLACE *(crosses to CARL)*. What?

CARL. You heard me. You're a whore.

EDGAR. Understand that it was just one time, Wallace. I'm not like that...

HOYT *(sarcastically)*. Thanks, Ed. I'm sure that makes him feel a lot better.

WALLACE. Shut up, Ed. You're a whore too. For once in your life admit that you're not any better than us.

EDGAR. What does that mean?

WALLACE. You're a cocksucker. No, you're a snob. You don't come up here to act like a kid, you come up here to make sure you're still better than the rest of us. So you can leave now, Ed. You're still smarter than us. You're still a better person than we are. And now you know that you've got a happier marriage. There's the door.

EDGAR. Is that what you think?

HOYT *(to WALLACE).* You're in no place to be showing people to the door. Why are you such a prick sometimes?

WALLACE. I was just getting to you, Hoyt. I oughta just go ahead and kick your ass.

HOYT. It's been a long time coming. I think you need to go home, Wallace. I think you need to go home and talk to Alice about fucking your friends, 'cause she's been doing it lately.

WALLACE. What do you mean lately?

HOYT. I mean me, Wallace. I mean the trip she made to Fayetteville a few weeks ago and how we fucked on my leather couch.

WALLACE. You son of a bitch! *(He charges HOYT, grabs him by the shirt and is about to hit him when EDGAR holds him back. WALLACE struggles and accidentally elbows EDGAR in the nose. EDGAR is knocked on the floor and WALLACE punches HOYT in the face. To EDGAR.)* Fuck you too. You sons of bitches are supposed to be my friends.

EDGAR. Goddammit, I think you broke my nose. *(Runs to the kitchen holding his nose. Begins wadding up paper towels, stuffing them in his nostrils to stop the bleeding.)*

CARL *(to HOYT on the floor).* You fucked Alice again? She has one goddamn affair and it's with you. I can't deal with this shit. *(Outburst.)* Why do I always get fucked over? I didn't even get a chance with her. *(CARL begins to gather up his things.)* You people... I'm through with y'all. I'm past you, Wallace. I'm beyond this shit. *(CARL searches for something else to say. He gives up and leaves.)*

WALLACE *(yelling sarcastically to the closed door).* It's all right, Carl. At least you didn't fuck her. My other friends here fucked her... Fucked my wife.

EDGAR *(adjusting the paper towels in his nose).* You know, I'm with Carl. I just can't do this anymore. I'm just not a part of this macho bullshit. I never have been. You're all such fucking... men. It's taken my whole life to realize that I'm not much of a man. I'm not. I don't like this shit. *(He gets his bag and packs up his things as WALLACE and HOYT watch him with blank stares.)* You were right, Wallace. I'm better than this. You guys gotta grow up. *(Pause.)* I...I'm sorry, guys.

(EDGAR leaves. WALLACE and HOYT are left in silence. They avoid eye contact, WALLACE then picks up his cooler and leaves without saying anything. HOYT goes to the refrigerator and gets two beers, one to drink and one to put on his sore face. He sits on the couch and drinks. WALLACE reenters with his cooler.)

WALLACE. Carl took the car. *(HOYT looks at him in silence. They avoid looking at each other. The tension and silence in the room eventually becomes unbearable. WALLACE sits on the other end of the couch. He pulls a beer out of his cooler, then puts it back.)* Can't we just fight or something? Settle this? I feel totally powerless.

HOYT. I don't know what to tell you, Wal. Would it help? Just go home. You've got a good wife. You both just fuck up a lot. Go home and apologize and tell her everything's forgiven.

WALLACE. I can't do that, Hoyt.

HOYT. Why not?

WALLACE. She was supposed to be better than me. She's not anymore. She's just like the rest of 'em. Besides, I'm...too much of a man. I like...this...shit, Hoyt. I can't apologize to her. It goes against everything I'm about.

HOYT. Then there's not much hope for you.

WALLACE. Yeah. I guess I just don't know any better.

HOYT. I...I'm sorry for my part in all this, Wallace.

WALLACE. Forget about it.

HOYT. No, it was a shitty thing for me to do.

WALLACE. I don't deny that.

HOYT. We're still animals, aren't we?

WALLACE. Let's not talk about it anymore. *(Pause.)* Are you gonna be able to take me home?

HOYT. Yeah, sure. You wanna go now?

WALLACE. No. *(Pause.)* I'm not ready yet. *(HOYT hands WALLACE the beer that he has been holding on his face. WALLACE opens it and they give each other a little toast, then stare out. John Prine's "Illegal Smile" starts. The stage goes to black.)*

END

ALL THINGS BEING EQUAL

Leonora B. Rianda
Oregon State University

"I don't want to achieve immortality through my work. I want to achieve immortality through not dying."

— Woody Allen

ALL THINGS BEING EQUAL

CHARACTERS

HELEN: The writer.
TROY: The corpse.
JANET: The janitor.

SETTING: *Bare stage except for a large manuscript thrown to one side of the stage with many of its pages torn out. Some of the pages are crumpled; some are ripped in half.*

AT RISE: *Music is heard*—"Mean to Me" (or producer's choice) *by Fred Ahlert and Roy Turk, sung by Linda Ronstadt, from her album* Lush Life. *TROY lies on the floor with a knife through his heart. HELEN is crouched next to him. Slowly, as the song ends, she stands, revealing blood on her hands, blouse and skirt.*

HELEN. Look at me! Ruined, all—ruined! *(Kicks TROY.)* Who's going to pay for this? Who's going to pay? My one good blouse, ruined! It kills me to think of it. As if I could afford dry-cleaning on what you pay me—what a waste. *(Takes off the blouse, throws it over TROY's face. She turns away from TROY and begins to collect the loose pages of the manuscript.)* All my life has come to this—a page here, a page there, and then in a moment, ruined—ruined. *(Starts crying as she collects the pages. She uncrumples one page, smoothes it out as best she can, and reads from it. Carefully, she un-sheathes the electric knife from its box near the oven and cuts her finger testing the sharpness of the blade. The taste of her own blood makes her sick to her stom-ach. She crumples the page and blows her nose in it.)*

TROY. So much violence—makes me sick. *(HELEN squeals, turns to face TROY who hasn't moved.)* So—gratuitous. Really. As if blood and guts could make up for a lack of passion.

HELEN. I killed you! I killed you!

TROY. All in vain—

HELEN *(delighted).* You're dead—you're dead!

TROY *(up on one elbow).* I vote we change the subject. Help me up.

HELEN *(goes back to collecting papers, sings).* "Ding-dong the witch is dead, the wicked witch, the wicked witch, ding-dong the wicked witch is dead"—

TROY *(throwing blouse at HELEN).* Help me up—please! My back is getting stiff.

HELEN. Please? Did you say please? I must be hearing things—

TROY. These hard surfaces, they kill me. Come on! Please! Please?

HELEN. You're dead—get used to it.

TROY. Oh God, oh God, spasm! Spasm! AAAhhh! *(HELEN, in alarm, quickly helps TROY to his feet. He straightens himself with difficulty. The knife protrudes from his chest.)* Weak back—my father. Same thing. Walk—gotta walk. *(He begins to pace back and forth.)*

HELEN. Can I get you anything? Some aspirin?

TROY. Nah, I just have to keep moving.

HELEN. Like a shark—

TROY. All my life I've had to be careful—nothing helps when it goes out—

HELEN. I had no idea about your back.

TROY. Obviously.

HELEN. You laughed. You laughed at me, Mr. Troy, getting back to the subject.

TROY. A joke, a joke! Where's your sense of humor, Helen?

HELEN. A sense of humor requires a big heart, Mr. Troy, a big heart and a generous imagination. There's so much you don't know about me. You shouldn't have touched what wasn't yours; you shouldn't have laughed, Mr. Troy.

TROY. I wasn't—well, OK, I laughed but really, you had nothing to do with it. I mean, don't take it personally, it's just that I was having such a rotten day and there I was and—there you were and—

HELEN (*holds up page to manuscript*). You grabbed my book. Touched it with your cold hands. Read out loud my words, my words in your mouth. Makes me sick to remember it.

TROY (*approaches HELEN*). Listen.

HELEN (*backs away*). Don't. Stay away. (*TROY and HELEN circle each other as they speak.*)

TROY. I want to explain something—listen.

HELEN (*mimics*). I want to explain something—listen.

TROY. I'm not going to apologize.

HELEN. I'm not going to apologize.

TROY. We're not getting anywhere like this—

HELEN. We're not getting anywhere—

TROY. Stop it.

HELEN. Stop it.

TROY. What are you doing?

HELEN. What are you doing?

TROY. My words—

HELEN. My words—

TROY. —your mouth

HELEN. —your mouth

TROY. That's it! Mouth to mouth—

HELEN. That's it! Mouth to mouth—

TROY. —resuscitation!

HELEN. You mean, regurgitation, don't you? *(They stop circling.)*

TROY. Three a.m.

HELEN. Three a.m.

TROY. Wide awake. Both of us. But we never said a word to each other.

HELEN. Not a word.

TROY. I couldn't hear her breathing. That's how I knew she was awake.

HELEN. That's how I knew.

TROY. There is nothing lonelier than that: to lie in the dark next to someone who is awake, who knows you are awake, but never says a word—waiting for each other to fall asleep so both of you can stop pretending you don't know the other one is awake. *(HELEN falls to her knees, grabs a piece of paper and starts scribbling.)*

HELEN. Go on, go on...but never says a word—waiting for each other to fall asleep—

TROY. Those are my words—

HELEN *(scribbling)*. —my words—

TROY. —in my mouth.

HELEN *(laughing)*. Yes, yes! Your tongue in my mouth. Don't stop now! Keep talking, keep talking. So—you woke up and then what, Mr. Troy? Did you kiss her?

TROY. My wife?

HELEN. Did you kiss her?

TROY. Helen, Helen—

HELEN *(scribbling)*. Mr. Troy kissed his wife on the mouth—she had stopped breathing.

TROY. You made that up—

HELEN. You kissed her—you must have kissed her. Loneliness that great requires emergency action. Mouth to mouth, no questions asked. Otherwise the heart stops beating. All is lost.

TROY. I'd like to get something off my chest—

HELEN. You kissed her—"bruised her mouth" as they say in the romances. Two people never just kiss, you know, enjoy anything so bland as mutual enjoyment— no, the hero must "bruise her mouth" or "crush her lips" because... well, he's always taller, for one thing...

TROY. What?

HELEN. I think it has something to do with being blond. Maybe there's less nerve ending in the lips of blondes—

TROY. Two things—stupid and stupid. I mean, what does height and hair color have to do with a man's ability to inflict injury on a woman's mouth? And—you read romances? I never would have thought—

HELEN. Love stories depress me. So I read romances. Now—you kissed her, right? *(Starts scribbling.)* Loneliness leads to desire leads to—

TROY (*starts circling again, slowly*). I got out of bed. Three a.m.—couldn't sleep, as I said. Stubbed my toe on the bedpost on my way to the bathroom.

HELEN (*stops writing, gets to her feet*). Three a.m. Couldn't sleep. Got out of bed. Made a large pot of coffee—

TROY (*grabs his toe, hops about on one foot*). Dammit dammit dammit dammit!

HELEN. I was so tired—poured myself a cup and drank—

TROY (*still hopping*). I hate that! Goddamm stupid stupid goddam bedpost—

HELEN. The coffee was scalding hot—

TROY (*demonstrating*). It hurt! So I kicked it, hard, with my other foot—

HELEN (*grabs her throat*). Aaahhh! My tongue—my throat—

TROY (*hopping on both feet*). My other toe! Ow ow ow ow—goddam goddam!

HELEN. I grabbed the ice tray from the freezer, slapped my tongue on it—aaaahhhh.

TROY. My wife started laughing—laughing and laughing—

HELEN (*as if tongue were stuck to ice tray*). My tongue— it stuck! I couldn't feel it anymore! I couldn't get it off the ice tray. I thought: I killed it!

TROY. I hated her—hated her laughing at me—

HELEN. I panicked—

TROY. My briefcase—I threw my briefcase at my wife who was laughing like a goddamm idiot—

HELEN. I tried to call 9-1-1. Help! Help! My tongue—my tongue!

TROY. Hit her right in the mouth.

HELEN. My tongue, I said, my tongue—stuck to the ice tray! But—the dispatcher couldn't understand me.

TROY. I split her lip—blood everywhere!

HELEN. Finally I thought, the shower, the shower! Hot water in my mouth. I pulled it off and it came back, the feeling in my tongue.

TROY. I apologized! My toes were throbbing, I thought they were broken and I apologized—

HELEN. I was so relieved—

TROY. And—she laughed—again. Blood everywhere, on the sheets, on her chin, her nightdress—her lip out to here like a badly parked motor home—

HELEN *(sticks her tongue out)*. It still hurts—can you see how red it is?

TROY. My toes are still killing me—do you mind if I take off my shoes?

HELEN. I wonder if my tongue will peel—shed its skin like a snake—more mature, better equipped and—did you know that snakes are completely blind during the shedding process?

TROY *(removes shoes)*. Aaahhhh...

HELEN. They'll strike at anything that comes near them—

TROY *(wiggling his toes)*. Maybe they're broken—

HELEN. Snakes smell with their tongues, you know—

TROY. Alas, I'll never dance again. *(Pause and then deliberately.)* "My broken toes corrupt my best attempts—"

HELEN. "My broken toes corrupt my best attempts—"

TROY. Don't start—

HELEN. No—iambic pentameter: My broken toes corrupt my best attempts— *(She falls to the floor. Starts scribbling.)* My broken toes corrupt my best attempts—

TROY (shrugs). Reveals how much I thought I didn't know—

HELEN (scribbling). Wait, wait!

TROY. I thought I could without remorse condemn—

HELEN. Go on, go on!

TROY. My way through life without a single woe—look. I've got a proposition—

HELEN. How'd you do that? Spontaneous iambic pentameter!

TROY. A lot of good it does me—

HELEN. Do you know how hard I struggle for a simple rhyme? For one effective metaphor? Just one moving passage that doesn't embarrass me—

TROY. If you wouldn't mind, there's something I'd like to propose—

HELEN. A poem. Just like that—just like *that*—

TROY. You see, I'm an artist too—

HELEN. No you're not—you're Mr. Corporation, Mr. Big Bucks, Mr. Sell Sell Sell, Mr. Take All You Can, Mr. Gotta Have Everything, Mr.—

TROY. Fine. Fine, you don't want to listen, then give me my words back—

HELEN. You're dead—what do you want with them?

TROY. They're mine.

HELEN. Mine. I killed you.

TROY. You can't do that—

HELEN. Sue me, Mr. Suddenly I'm an Artist.

TROY. A heart to heart, you and me.

HELEN. That's impossible. We've nothing to say to each other.

TROY. Nine years we've worked together—a few minutes more, what's your hurry?

HELEN (*collecting her manuscript off the floor*). I'm not listening if I can't use what I hear.

TROY. Then I'm not talking if I can't keep what I say.

HELEN. There you have it—we're nothing to each other. Not listening, not talking. We're dead to each other. I don't have much time—I'd like to get home, clean up a little before they surround my house with a SWAT team.

TROY (*jumps around*). Look—rigor mortis hasn't even set in yet. I'm 'flexive! I'd like to explain—

HELEN. There's nothing to explain. After nine years of working for you, I stabbed you in the heart with a letter opener. Nothing personal except that you surprised me. Showed up when I didn't expect you—and there I was, in the middle of a paragraph where I had finally worked up the courage to have the bastard when suddenly you lean over my shoulder, laugh at what I had written and then grab—without asking—my manuscript in your thick, grimy fingers. Grab it, just like that, without asking me if you may touch it. Laughing. Laughing at my work.

TROY. I'm sure it was a typo—

HELEN. What?

TROY. I leaned over your shoulder and read, "...throwing the knife aside, she grabbed the *bun* and shot him twice." "Bun." You wrote "bun."

HELEN. Bun?

TROY. Hamburger, hot dog? I couldn't help but wonder...

HELEN. That's why you laughed? Because I typed "bun" instead of "gun"?

TROY. I was curious—I had to go back, catch up, find out where things had gone wrong, that's why I grabbed your manuscript—was "bun" intentional? Was "bun" what you really wanted to say? Had I stumbled into The Divine Comedy or a translation of Samuel Beckett?

HELEN. I killed you because of a typo?

TROY. Well, to be completely honest, I was laughing at you— I mean, you should have seen the look on your face when I walked in—surprise!! It was almost worth losing my life just to see you do that with your face— like someone's home movies run backwards at triple speed. You made me laugh!

HELEN. As if it were a joy to work for you—not once, not in nine years, did you ever say, "please" or "thank you" or "how are you today, Helen?" Not—once. Not once. Mr. Troy enters office: "Grunt, grunt, grunt. Do this, Helen, do that. Grunt, grunt, grunt."

TROY. You hated me.

HELEN. That's not why I killed you.

TROY. You shouldn't have taken my indifference so personally—do I take it personally that you hate my guts?

HELEN. Your guts aren't the issue. You have no heart.

TROY. Now you're getting personal.

HELEN (beams). There! Better? Is this what you wanted?

TROY. That's grotesque.

HELEN (still beaming). Go ahead, ask me. Say "Helen, how are *you* today?"

TROY (falsely, awkwardly). Helen, how are you—today? Please.

HELEN. Grotesque.

TROY. I'm new at this—

HELEN. Neither one of us— (Pause.)

TROY. For nine years we worked like this—

HELEN. A change of heart?

TROY. We can't change history.

HELEN. But we can change the way we choose to tell it...

TROY. A change of heart? You and I, together, like two pieces of fruit ripening slowly in the same bowl.

HELEN *(excited, scribbles).* I like that! Two-pieces-of-fruit— How come I never heard any of this stuff from you when you were alive? It's great!

TROY. I wanted to—I was—afraid.

HELEN. Ripening-slowly-in-the-same-bowl. Say something else.

TROY. Listen! Do you hear it?

HELEN *(suspicious).* The sound of ripening fruit?

TROY. Listen! Big Band music! I love this stuff! Listen, listen! *(He starts swaying to unheard music.)* I always wanted to take dance lessons.

HELEN. I thought we were getting somewhere.

TROY. When I was a kid, I begged my mother for dance lessons. An Arthur "Murky" studio was just down the street—*"please, Ma!"* She laughed at me. "Dance lessons," she said, "dance lessons? I work like a horse all day long—even your brother has a paper route—and *you* want to take dance lessons? We work so you can dance? My feet are killing me, I have a varicose vein the size of Texas that won't stop throbbing—my back is broken. I'm so tired. And you want me to pay some Big-Shot Twinkle Toes to give *you* dance lessons?" *(Pause.)* A simple "no" would have been enough, I think, I'm not some kind of monster.

HELEN *(frustrated).* *I* can't hear the music!

TROY. She worked very hard, my mother. Waitressed. Cleaned houses. Her legs would swell up—her ankles were red and swollen—the bottoms of her feet, chapped—yellow like old parchment.

HELEN. Wait! That was good— *(Scribbles.)* "yellow-like-old-parchment."

TROY. At night she'd peel off her support hose and soak her feet—it made me sick to watch her. I couldn't eat for hours.

HELEN. My father—he loved to dance. World War II, he said, was the best time for dance music. Young men off to die, young women dying to break hearts. Every night before I went to bed, he'd put on the Andrews Sisters— he was a strong lead, my father, he knew all the right moves. My mother always left the room when we started dancing.

TROY. Tommy "Drosey." Nelson Riddle. Benny Goodman. Harry James. Kids at school were listening to the Beatles but I was listening to Big Band!

HELEN. There! I hear it! I hear it!

TROY. Boogie-Woogie Bugle Boy!

HELEN. Yes! *(Sings.)* "He was soooome Boogie-Woogie Bugle Boy of Company B!"

TROY. Dance with me!

TROY & HELEN. "He's in the Army now, blowing reveille— He was some Boogie-Woogie Bugle Boy of Company B!" *(TROY and HELEN start boogying to invisible swing music. They never miss a beat. Together, their timing is perfect...until TROY dips HELEN.)*

HELEN. Ow!

TROY. Ow! My back!

HELEN. You hurt me!

TROY. I'm so clumsy, I'm sorry—ah, I've pulled something. Come on, let's dance, it's almost over.

HELEN. Ow, my heart!

TROY. I'm sorry, I'm sorry, I'm sorry—please?! The music—

HELEN. No! You hurt me!

TROY. I said *please!* Come on!

HELEN. You could have killed me! Get away from me!

TROY. I want to dance!

HELEN. So dance! You don't need me—

TROY. I *want* you—please!

HELEN. I've got two left feet. Go ahead, dance!

TROY. Not by myself.

HELEN. Gene Kelly, Fred Astaire—they didn't need partners—

TROY. They were stars—no one laughed at them. Please please please, I feel *so alive!* I could dance all night!

HELEN. My father never asked—he just expected me to follow his lead. It made me sick, waiting every night for the music to start.

TROY. I'll be careful, I promise—

HELEN. You're dead...you're dead. I killed you.

TROY. But the music—

HELEN. I don't hear the music anymore—

TROY. I do— I'll hear it for both of us—please!

HELEN. Don't you know when to quit? I'm *not* dancing.

TROY. The music, it's fading away—

HELEN. I'll step on your toes, you'll get angry.

TROY. I can barely hear it—

HELEN. The party's over—time to go home.

TROY. Gone. It's gone.

HELEN. My father, he liked to dip me over at the end of a song—the last time he had a heart attack. Fell right on top of me. I couldn't breathe—

TROY (*distracted*). An avalanche of fatherly love.

HELEN. Yes—yes! (*Scribbling.*) "An-avalanche-of-fa-therly-love."

TROY. Buried alive. (*Pause.*) Welcome to the surface.

HELEN. My first deep breath in years.

TROY. We'll hum something—dance with me.

HELEN. My manuscript—we've stepped all over it. What a mess. (*She starts to collect it.*)

TROY. The music is over.

HELEN. It's finally finished—my only consolation is the time I have left to rewrite.

TROY. Let me help you

HELEN. No—don't touch it! You don't know what order it goes in!

TROY. I can help you!

HELEN. No! You'll tell me what to do!

TROY. Don't do this to me—

HELEN. See? "Don't do this, don't do that—" Please. All my life, my heart has been the last thing on my mind. (*Their hands touch on the same piece of paper.*) I've been nothing to you. And now, all of a sudden, you want something from me—something—unprofessional. Unbusinesslike.

TROY. If you leave now, I'm finished. You're finished. I can help you.

HELEN (*gently takes the piece of paper*). This is very awkward. (*Continues to pick up paper.*) Really, there's nothing I want from you.

TROY. Yes there is—

HELEN. What?

TROY. I don't know, I don't know, but it's like this: when you're dreaming—and you know you're dreaming—

when suddenly the rules of the Earth no longer apply to you—when the freedom of being in a dream comes to you and the sky's the limit—you run, you jump into the air and know that during this time alone there isn't any place you can't get to—it's absurd and exhilarating. It's heartbreaking, it's so beautiful. I'm in this dream, you see, and you're with me. There are things to be said for this— I want to say them. Before oblivion destroys me.

HELEN. I'm the other woman.

TROY. My wife will be shocked—and then, pleasantly surprised that I'm no longer coming home.

HELEN. I'm the Angel of Mercy.

TROY. Grant me eternity then—a decent ending. Not this—a sordid bloody mess.

HELEN. You're a very interesting man—for a corpse, I mean.

TROY. I want to tell you things—

HELEN. No confessions! No confessions—

TROY. My only hope is you—

HELEN. And what hope do I have?

TROY. I can be your muse.

HELEN. My muse. How amusing. My luck. You're standing on my work.

TROY. I'll make it up to you.

HELEN. For nine years you've either ignored me or acknowledged my existence only because you needed something. I didn't really care, I mean, this place meant nothing to me except as a source of income—a dream, this place was, a nightmare. Sure, there were moments when my body responded to yours—when you would stand behind me reaching over my shoulder for something on my desk—once, you actually smiled at me, well, maybe it wasn't exactly, probably my face just got in the way, but I liked to imagine it was me you meant to flatter.

TROY. A double life—a family I couldn't trust, a job I couldn't stand. I wanted to dance—

HELEN. Two left feet, that's me.

TROY. No dignity. No integrity.

HELEN. You laughed at my work—you threw my manuscript all over the office. As a muse, your technique stinks.

TROY. My life is in your hands—please. Don't destroy me.

HELEN. The power is—

TROY. —yours—yours—all yours.

HELEN. A heady feeling.

TROY. But the heart of the matter is this: iambic pentameter, metaphor, image, theme. I'm a natural.

HELEN. Out of the rubble arises the Phoenix.

TROY. You are the Phoenix.

HELEN. I am the rubble.

TROY. Together, we can create a whole new world—

HELEN. —out of dead matter...

TROY. What does it matter? Don't you see it? Don't you feel it? Smell it? Want it?

HELEN. Nothing matters to you except how this all ends.

TROY. Yes—no! OK, why not? But I could guarantee you immortality—together, we'll be immortal.

HELEN. My book. My manuscript. The instrument of your salvation—and you laughed. Threw it on the ground. Told me I was fired for using company property for personal reasons.

TROY. Take it from me. As it is, you've got nothing.

HELEN. Nothing?

TROY. A great start, sure, but there's no music—

HELEN. Two left feet—

TROY. Wait. Don't tell me off until the last chapter—and then we'll live as one, together, forever!

HELEN. I can't wait that long to kill you off— There is no grace period—

TROY. Then it cannot live—

HELEN. How do you know, how do you know?

TROY. The advantage is mine—from where I stand, the view is limitless. *(He steps on top of HELEN's manuscript. Shades his eyes.)* If your heart is in it, there's nothing that cannot be revealed. Helen, the world is at my feet—and yours, too, if you'll let me help you. *(HELEN gently pushes TROY off the manuscript. She bends over to pick it up, then changes her mind and straightens. She looks at TROY who offers his hand. She steps on top of her manuscript and, like TROY, shades her eyes, as if the sun were too bright.)*

HELEN. "Look, Ma! Top of the world!" Wow. It's so— clear from up here. Look, look! My house—there's my house! And there's the freeway I take every single god-damned morning to work for nine years! *(Pause.)* Uh-oh. Altitude. *(Tilts head back.)* Nosebleed! Oh, not now, not now—oh. Oh. OK. There. Maybe not. OK, I'm just lightheaded, afraid of heights, or, when I'm up so high, I wonder what it would be like to jump. To fall. From so high a place. I'm attracted to the edge, you know. Closer, closer—a little closer. There is nothing to grab on to—nothing, just the sheer edge and then—aaaaaahhhhhh! *(Pause.)* Does one—faint—before impact? Imagine being conscious, smashing into the earth—the body—the body—meeting absolute resistance? *(Pause.)* Mmmmmm, smell the air up here! So clean and fresh—beyond their pollution, their noise, their—needs. Uh-oh, dizzy. Breathe! Breathe. Relax. Mmmmmm. *(Pause.)* I've been coming up here for all the years of my life. Today that makes forty. Today I am forty years old. Of course, when I was very young, my father used to bring me up here. Only the altitude would make him irritable. He'd point out targets below and see if he could hit them with rocks. "See that weed over there," he'd say, "I'm gonna hit it with this rock!" All I could see was a large wildflower, orange like a rising sun. I thought it was beautiful. "Watch!" he'd say. Zing! I have to admit, he was pretty good. At that distance he could knock off quite a few petals—a skinny stem left shivering in the clear clean air. Then he'd point out to me where he worked, tell me again how much he hated it, how much he hated all the stupid, sheepy people he had to work with, how he was trapped—then he'd pick up really big rocks and heave them into the air. "Thunk." Like a body hitting the earth, "thunk." Those rocks made such a hollow, heavy sound. "Thunk." Even before he died, I learned my way up here so I could be alone. The older I get, the harder the climb. And today, it's forty years of climbing. Look! Look how clear it is today. This is how Noah must have felt after forty nights, forty days of rain—to at last come to rest on the earth again. Looking around and everything clean and fresh and all his, all his! To populate! To go forth and multiply! What a job! What a great job! To create and create and create, morning, noon and night! Imagine! Surveying all that lies below and knowing it's yours, all yours. That God is *definitely* on your side—there being no other side for Him to take— Forty years and here I am. Dry land at last. The ark has come to rest. My body touches the earth. And now what? Do I throw rocks or go forth and multiply? The fast way down is over the edge. *(Balances on one foot.)* "Look, Ma! No hands!" *(Pause.)* In the brief time it takes to fall, I imagine I am flying!

TROY. My Angel of Mercy falls out of heaven.

HELEN. She is pushed—off balance—by those around her scrambling for a foothold.

TROY *(offers his hand)*. Let me help you.

(Enter JANET the JANITOR.)

JANET. Tsk, tsk—such a mess! *(She sees TROY and gasps.)*

HELEN *(to JANET)*. Let me help you—

JANET. The sight of blood—

TROY. She's going to faint—

HELEN. I won't hurt you—

JANET. The sight of blood— *(JANET falls to the ground in a faint.)*

TROY *(stands over her)*. Two's company, three's a crowd.

HELEN. She's seen the blood on my hands—

TROY. We're doomed. She's seen your work here tonight.

HELEN *(frantically gathering up her manuscript)*. It's begun, it's begun. I'm finished, I'm finished.

TROY *(kneeling beside HELEN)*. She's seen your work here tonight. She'll turn you in.

HELEN. I want to go home. I want to put these pages in order before they come to get me.

TROY. No one knows you're here.

HELEN. *She* does—Janet! And this isn't the first time, Mr. Troy. She knows who I am. We've talked sometimes, late at night when I was here working—

TROY. You left every night promptly at five. Every night.

HELEN. Of course I left, of course I did. All day long, going through the motions. All day long, dreaming of night when I could return to write my book. After you had gone. After everyone had left. I returned. During the day this place was my coffin. At five p.m. I was free to come back and roam the world looking looking looking for fresh blood to add to my story.

TROY. I had no idea.

HELEN. My heart was in it, then, on those nights—like tonight, before—

TROY. Listen. Listen, I told my wife that I had board meetings every Thursday night.

JANET *(rising on one elbow)*. Mr. Troy—such a beautiful dancer.

TROY. One night a week I was a prince—

JANET. And I was Cinderella in a beautiful dress at the ball—

TROY. Ballroom dancing at the YMCA. My wife had no idea—

JANET. Such a beautiful dancer, Mr. Troy. And I worked nights cleaning offices so I could afford dance lessons.

TROY. Janet and I, we—let's show her.

JANET. She wouldn't understand— *(TROY helps JANET to her feet. Together they waltz around the room. Their dance is slow, passionate. They never take their eyes off of each other. They are oblivious to anything else.)*

HELEN. Excuse me, you're stepping all over my work. *(Tries to retrieve the pages of her manuscript from beneath the feet of the dancing couple. She finally gathers up the rest of the pages. She puts on her coat, stuffs her manuscript in a sack, grabs her purse and heads for the door. TROY sees her and stops dancing. He leaves JANET and rushes to HELEN.)*

TROY. Hey hey! Don't go!

JANET. Mr. Troy, the music—it's our favorite song.

TROY. Helen, don't go!

HELEN. Why did you stop?

TROY. I want to go with you.

HELEN. What about her, what about Janet?

JANET. Mr. Troy, Mr. Troy—one more dance, please. Oscar, he's a sweet man, the only man I've ever loved. But he can't dance, arthritis in both feet. Every night I soak his feet, massage each foot as if it were a poor deformed baby—one night a week.

TROY *(to HELEN).* This state carries the death penalty you know. How long do you think you're going to last?

HELEN. This state? The death penalty?

TROY. The present administration is eager to set an example. And I gave them lots of money to stay in power. The death penalty—

JANET. Lethal injection—collapses the lungs, arrests the heart. Troy, listen—the rumba! *(Starts dancing alone.)*

TROY. If you don't stop her, you're finished.

JANET. Dance with me, Mr. Troy!

TROY. You've killed once, you can kill again. Otherwise, you're doomed. She's seen your work here.

HELEN. She has seen the blood on my hands—

TROY. This state caries the death penalty—

HELEN. So you're suggesting—

TROY. Snuff her out!!

JANET (*dancing with an imaginary partner*). I could dance all night!

HELEN. Look at me, covered with blood!

TROY. Look at me! If you get caught, I'm a goner, a goner!

HELEN. I'll have lots of time to write after they throw me in prison. All day long with nothing to do but write. No meals to cook, no laundry to wash, no rent to pay. I'll have lots of time—

TROY. They'll make an example of you. There isn't enough time—

HELEN. Don't rush me, don't rush me—

TROY. You'll be fried before you're finished—take care of Janet so you can go on living.

HELEN. You only want me for my body of work—

TROY. I'm a dead man, what can I say?

HELEN. I won't do it. No more sacrifices. I'm done here. I'm going.

TROY. Did I tell you about the time my boy threatened to kill me? Said I was a monster and he was going to kill me? He was nine years old. I hit my wife once when he was in the room. (*JANET stops dancing and lies down on the floor where she fainted. She lies still.*)

HELEN. And this will change all that? I can't change that—the damage is done. You're going to have to live with it.

TROY. Helen, your book is nothing without me. Listen— listen. See, the future's here in my head, now, as we speak. Put me in your book—of course, change the names to protect the innocent—and I swear you'll live forever. You and I. I have something to give—to give you. My life comes to nothing unless you kill me off in the last chapter. Your life's work comes to nothing unless you take me with you. My family, for one, will love the ending—I guarantee you. It's the least I could do— It's the greatest thing that you could do. Please?

HELEN. OK. Janet lives—you die. Last chapter. That's my final offer.

TROY. Yes, I'm grateful. Really I am—

HELEN *(nudges JANET with her foot).* She'll be doing me a favor.

TROY. I can help you. I'll follow you, everywhere—

HELEN. I could use the company. Sometimes I'm so lonely I can't remember where I am—

TROY. Let me help you.

HELEN *(hands TROY the manuscript).* Would you carry this for me?

TROY. I'd be honored. *(HELEN leaves first. TROY follows, but turns with the manuscript in his arms. He turns off the light and closes the door quietly. Lights out. Music: "Skylark" by Hoagy Carmichael, or producer's choice.)*

END

THE FATHER CLOCK

Walter Wykes
University of Nevada, Las Vegas

CHARACTERS

SNUB: A young man.
FLUB: An older man.
STAGE MANAGER: A woman.

PLACE: A theatre.

TIME: The present.

THE FATHER CLOCK premiered at the University of Nevada, Las Vegas, on October 29, 1997 with the following cast:

Flub . . . . DOUG HILL
Snub . . . . RUSS MARCHAND
Stage Manager . . . . SHEILAGH M. POLK

The production was directed and designed by Greg Vovos with sound design by Matt Moore.

THE FATHER CLOCK

NOTE: <> indicates lines of dialogue that belong to the play within the play.

SETTING: *A bare stage. Shadows from the grid above. Somewhere, the ticking of a clock. After a few moments, a dim glow appears DC and grows into a great pool of light. Silence except for the ticking of the clock. More silence. Finally frantic whispering offstage L.*

FLUB. Where is she?
SNUB. What?
FLUB. Where is she?
SNUB. Who?
FLUB. The stage manager! *(The whispering rises, grows indecipherable. A heated exchange. A slap.)*
SNUB. Oww!

(Pause. FLUB rushes across the stage, his face hidden beneath his jacket. He disappears into the wings, R. More whispering, urgent but indecipherable.)

STAGE MANAGER. Breathe! *(Offstage R, FLUB takes in a great gulp of air.)* Now go!
FLUB. But—
STAGE MANAGER. Go!
FLUB. All right! I don't think they suspect anything yet!

(Again, FLUB rushes across the stage, his jacket over his head. He disappears into the wings, L.)

FLUB. She's coming!
SNUB. What?
FLUB. She's coming!
SNUB. So?

(Another heated exchange as the STAGE MANAGER enters and steps into the pool of light. She is an attractive young woman, although a little out of sorts. Offstage, a slap.)

FLUB. Oww!
STAGE MANAGER. Good evening, and welcome to— *(She sneezes.)* Sorry. There's...ahh...there's something going around. A little bug. *(She wipes her nose.)* Welcome to the theatre. Now, before we get started, I'm afraid we have a bit of bad news. The director won't be with us tonight. He was called away suddenly. Several weeks ago. *(Pause.)* Before rehearsals began, really. *(Pause.)* Oh, no need to worry! I know many of you have come for his fabled *mise en scène*, and you won't be disappointed! He did supervise some table work! And we do have *this*— *(She produces a black prompt book.)* —with a few scribbles from the director himself! Various notes. Suggestions and so forth. So stay for the show. We think you'll find his hand at work in our little play. And if you must leave, please slip out as quietly as possible. Without making too much of a fuss. The actors, you know. *(Lights shift.)* OK. That's it. *(She sneezes, takes her place on a stool R, and flips to the*

beginning of the prompt book.) The home of Flub and Snub Drub. Four walls—deep olive.

(Lights rise to full on the empty stage.)

Note from the director: Four walls may or may not appear. Probably not. *(They do not.)* A table R. Two chairs.

(FLUB enters with a table and two chairs. SNUB wanders on behind him, casuallly smoking a cigarette. FLUB drops his load R and carefully places each item in its proper place. SNUB flops down in one of the chairs. FLUB glares at him.)

A couch.

(FLUB turns to exit. He pauses for a moment, expecting SNUB to follow, but he does not. Exit FLUB, glaring. He returns with a couch.)

Brown.

(As FLUB's couch is not brown, he exits. He returns with a brown couch.)

With four legs.

(As FLUB's couch has only three legs, he exits. He returns with a brown, four-legged couch.)

Stage left.

(FLUB complies. SNUB puffs on his cigarette. The STAGE MANAGER watches carefully. When FLUB is finished, she continues.)

A purple throw rug from Indonesia just downstage and to the right of the couch.

(FLUB glares at SNUB. He motions, "After you," but SNUB does not budge. Again, he motions, "After you." Again, SNUB does not budge. FLUB exits in a huff. He produces the rug and, with a flourish, places it in front of the couch.)

A grandfather clock, upstage center.

(Exit FLUB. Offstage, a tremendous groan. FLUB re-appears carrying a huge antique grandfather clock and places it UC. The clock has no hands, but its pendulum is in motion and its steady ticking fills the auditorium.)

This particular piece was procured by the director himself!

SNUB. Pfff. *(SNUB exits. The others glare after him.)*
STAGE MANAGER. Snub Drub enters as if from nowhere.

(SNUB enters—clearly from somewhere. He may be clawing his way out of some primordial muck, blowing kisses to a lover he has just left behind, running from some mythical beast with four heads and ten eyes, or perhaps all of these at once.)

STAGE MANAGER. From nowhere. *(SNUB shrugs his shoulders and snorts.)* From *nowhere. (SNUB ignores her, or perhaps continues his pantomime.)* Snub Drub enters as if—

SNUB *(nastily)*. Trollop!

STAGE MANAGER. *What's that?*

SNUB. Pig-whore! *(SNUB folds his arms and turns away from the STAGE MANAGER. She approaches him.)*

STAGE MANAGER. Is there a *problem?*

SNUB. No!

STAGE MANAGER. *No? No problem? (SNUB ignores her.)* Then what was all of *this? (She reenacts his entrance. SNUB shrugs.)*

SNUB. Nothing.

STAGE MANAGER. *Nothing?*

SNUB. I'm trying to establish the "moment before."

STAGE MANAGER. Ahh! The moment before!

SNUB. That's right.

STAGE MANAGER. Well, that's very considerate. But the note specifically states— *(SNUB snorts and rolls his eyes.)* All right. That's enough. Snub Drub enters as if—

SNUB *(explodes)*. Why? Why do I have to enter from *nowhere?* What if I want to enter from *somewhere?*

STAGE MANAGER. It's not your place to question.

SNUB. Why not?

STAGE MANAGER. An actor doesn't have to understand.

SNUB. Why not?

STAGE MANAGER. It's not his place.

SNUB. Why not?

STAGE MANAGER. Because!

SNUB. Because *why?*

STAGE MANAGER. It's the director's job!

SNUB. Ah-hah! The *director!* I knew it'd come down to him!

STAGE MANAGER. Oh, just do it. We don't have time for—

SNUB. But it doesn't make any sense! Think about it! The way you used to! Take the whole clock thing—

STAGE MANAGER. Don't!

SNUB. Break it down!

STAGE MANAGER. Don't start about the clock! From nowhere!

SNUB. There's no logical explanation!

STAGE MANAGER. It's symbolic!

SNUB. Of what? *(Pause.)*

STAGE MANAGER. From nowhere!

SNUB. You see! It doesn't make any—

STAGE MANAGER *(reading from the prompt book).* Note from the Director: It is most crucial that Snub enter as if from nowhere! Nothingness! Absolute non-existence! The fact that he is, indeed, entering from somewhere is irrelevant! Total nonsense! The important thing is that he's here!

(They glare at each other for a long moment. Finally, SNUB relents. He exits and returns a moment later as if from nowhere.)

Thank you.

SNUB *(under his breath).* He's lost his mind.

STAGE MANAGER. What's that?

SNUB. Nothing. *(Pause. The STAGE MANAGER returns to her prompt book.)*

STAGE MANAGER. Snub wears a pleasant expression, although not so pleasant! A raspberry longing in his eyes. His hair is short and hangs to his waist. He is well built, although a little flabby and thin as a stick. His dress is not unusual. And he carries with him an ice cream cone—flavor optional. *(SNUB produces an ice cream cone.)* He flops down on the couch. Head stage right. Feet stage left. Belly up. One foot off. Cone in downstage hand. *(SNUB complies.)* Enter Flub Drub. He wheezes slightly.

(Enter FLUB, wheezing.)

Approximately ten decibels please. *(FLUB complies.)* He looks much the same as Snub—only older. In his left hand, he carries a pipe. *(FLUB produces a pipe.)*

FLUB. <Snub...I call you Snub because that is your name. Snub Drub.>

STAGE MANAGER. Snub licks his cone.

FLUB. <As you well know...I am your father.>

STAGE MANAGER. Snub licks his cone! *(He does.)*

FLUB. <Please do not drip on this couch which we purchased only yesterday at approximately two a.m. in the freezing blizzard that is outside our prefabricated home in the northern portion of the United States of America—specifically North Dakota—although we are originally from Amarillo.>

STAGE MANAGER. A strange expression comes over Snub that cannot be explained. *(Indeed, it does.)*

FLUB. <Son?>

SNUB. <Our couch!>

FLUB. <What's that?>

SNUB. <Our couch! Our couch!>

FLUB. <Ahh! Yes!>

SNUB. <I remember!>

FLUB. <The couch?>

SNUB. <The old one!>

FLUB. <Ahh! The old one!>

SNUB. <I remember when we bought it!>

FLUB. <Yesterday. When you were six.>

SNUB. <We went to the store—>

FLUB. <The store! That's right!>

SNUB. <—and we bought the couch!>

FLUB. <We bought it! Yes!>

SNUB. <You said, "Snub, do you think this couch will do?" And I said, "Yes, Father," for you are my father, "I think it will." I remember quite vividly. It was also brown—>

FLUB. <Like broccoli.>

SNUB. <—although not as comfortable.>

FLUB. <And with only three legs.>

SNUB. <My mother—your wife—who is now dead if you don't remember—loved that couch.> *(The STAGE MANAGER sneezes. FLUB and SNUB stare at her. She wipes her nose.)*

STAGE MANAGER. Oh...sorry...sorry...go ahead...I'm sorry...go on...just a little cold.

SNUB *(bitterly)*. Hah! A little cold!

FLUB. What's that she says?

SNUB. A cold!

FLUB. A cold! Ah!

SNUB. Strumpet!

FLUB. Trollop!

SNUB. Hussy!

FLUB. Wench!

SNUB. Where do you suppose she *caught* that cold?

FLUB. That cold?

SNUB. Yes! "The cold!"

FLUB. Hmmm...let me think!

SNUB. The *old?*

FLUB. The *dying?*

SNUB. The *sick?*

FLUB. *Diseased?*

SNUB. Perhaps she shouldn't hump the lepers! Bang the bedridden!

STAGE MANAGER. It's just a little cold!

SNUB. A little cold, she says!

FLUB. Hah! A little cold!

STAGE MANAGER. DO YOU MIND?

SNUB (*to FLUB, quietly*). A short temper. That's one of the first signs.

STAGE MANAGER. All right! That's it! Perhaps you'd like to muddle through on your own! Perhaps I should just take the book and leave!

FLUB. No, wait—

SNUB. Go ahead. (*SNUB pulls a cigarette from his pocket and lights up.*) Take the clock too, if you'd like. It's only confusing things.

STAGE MANAGER. Oh! *It's* confusing things?

SNUB. That's right.

FLUB. He's...he's only saying that. He doesn't mean it. *Do you?* He's really quite fond of the clock. He's confided in me many times just how...how fond of it he is.

How it comforts him! Nurtures him! Suckles him like a pig! *(SNUB snorts.)* It's just...it's just...with his hard outer shell...you know...it's so hard for him to admit.

SNUB. We're better off without it.

FLUB. Shut up!

SNUB. Well, it's true.

FLUB. No need to take chances!

STAGE MANAGER. No smoking.

SNUB. What's that?

STAGE MANAGER. No smoking in the theatre.

SNUB. You never complained when *he* used to light up.

STAGE MANAGER. It was his theatre.

SNUB *(jumps on this)*. Was? Did you say *was?*

STAGE MANAGER *(flustered)*. No...I—

SNUB. "Was!" "Was his theatre!"

FLUB. We...we should continue! OK? Here...here we go! We're moving on! We're...we're, ahh...c'mon... we're...we're not... *(Pause.)* What would he think if he were to return and find us like this? He could be making his way through the parking lot right now! Wiping the smoke and dust from his spectacles! He...he could be in the lobby...his ear pressed to the door...listening! He'd be heartbroken! And besides... *(FLUB glances nervously into the auditorium.)* I think they're getting restless! *(All three turn to the audience. An awkward pause.)*

STAGE MANAGER. You're right. *(STAGE MANAGER flips through her prompt book. FLUB moves back to his place, SNUB takes a deep drag.)* Snub extinguishes his cigarette.

SNUB. It doesn't say—

STAGE MANAGER. Snub extinguishes his cigarette! *(Pause.)*

SNUB. Fine. *(He extinguishes the cigarette and returns to his place.)* That's all you understand anymore. Rules.

FLUB *(continuing the performance)*. <As you know, Snub, I have called you here under the premise of purchasing yet a third couch. Of course, I am slightly untrustworthy, as you know, and there is the possibility this was a ruse.>

SNUB. <That is always a possibility with you, Father. As you say, you are slightly untrustworthy.>

FLUB. <Indeed.>

SNUB. <Take, for instance, the time you told me we were going to the fair and instead you took me for a polio vaccination.>

FLUB. <Ah! Yes!> (FLUB laughs *maniacally.*)

SNUB. <Or the spoon thing.> (FLUB freezes.)

STAGE MANAGER. An awkward moment. *(Indeed.)*

FLUB. <As...as you know, your mother—who is dead—>

SNUB. <What did she die of again?>

FLUB. <Polio.>

SNUB. <That's right. Do you remember when we bought this clock?>

FLUB. <Ah! The Father Clock!>

SNUB. <There was a saleswoman with dark red lipstick and large thighs. She wore a purple blouse.>

FLUB. <Yes! She gave you that cone!>

SNUB. <A black skirt. And her panty-line was quite visible. I remember noticing her panty-line. It was an important moment in my life. A sexual awakening, if you will.>

STAGE MANAGER. The clock strikes five. *(Indeed, it does. At the sound of the clock, FLUB and SNUB exchange positions on the stage. Each attempts to replicate the other actor's last posture exactly. FLUB now holds the cone. SNUB holds the pipe.)*

SNUB *(mimics FLUB)*. <Yes...she reminded me of your mother...who is dead.>

FLUB *(mimics SNUB)*. <What did she die of again?>

SNUB. <Polio.>

FLUB. <That's right.>

SNUB. <As you know, I have been alone all these years since your dear mother—who is dead—died. Well...feeling lonely, and having no outlet for my ravenous sexual desires, I have decided to remarry.>

FLUB. <Won't mother be jealous?>

SNUB. <Don't be ridiculous. She has her theatrical career.>

FLUB. <That's true.>

SNUB. <She's getting rave reviews!>

FLUB. <Yes...I've heard.>

SNUB. <Actually, I have remarried several times since her demise—although I never told you.>

FLUB. <Indeed?>

SNUB. <Truly.>

FLUB. <Who will you marry this time, Father? I ask, although I am thrown slightly off balance by your sudden announcement.>

SNUB. <The woman who sold us the clock. With the red lipstick and the panty-line.>

STAGE MANAGER. A strange contortion flits across Flub's mackle. *(Pause.)*

FLUB *(to STAGE MANAGER)*. What's that?

STAGE MANAGER. A strange contortion flits across Flub's mackle.

FLUB. Mackle?

STAGE MANAGER. Mackle.

FLUB. You're certain? (*STAGE MANAGER scrunches up her nose, presses the prompt book to her face.*)

STAGE MANAGER. Yes. Mackle.

SNUB (*to STAGE MANAGER*). He's lost his mind. I told you.

FLUB. Let me see.

SNUB. I warned you, but you wouldn't listen.

STAGE MANAGER. Mackle.

SNUB. It's finally spread to his brain. (*STAGE MANAGER sneezes.*)

FLUB. Hmmm...

STAGE MANAGER. Flits across his mackle!

SNUB. He's probably wandered off in a blind stupor. *That's* where he is. He's probably sitting on a corner somewhere, drooling on his trousers, babbling nonsense and—

FLUB. Shhh! What are you—

SNUB. —and if I recall correctly, it all started with a little cold! (*The STAGE MANAGER sneezes.*) Bless you. (*SNUB and FLUB stare at her. She wipes her nose.*)

STAGE MANAGER. You're jealous!

FLUB (*extremely agitated*). Yes! Jealous!

SNUB. Hah!

STAGE MANAGER. You're such a child sometimes.

FLUB. Yes! A child!

STAGE MANAGER. You don't understand the way things are at all.

FLUB. Not at all!

SNUB. A *child?*

STAGE MANAGER. That's right.

FLUB. He ... he was called away! *Remember?*

SNUB. Trollop!

FLUB *(offers SNUB the prompt book, a distraction).* What ... ahh—

SNUB. Jezebel!

FLUB. What do you make of this? This here. *(FLUB shoves the book at SNUB.)* It's handwritten. Encrypted. Takes a precise eye. *(As SNUB leans reluctantly over the prompt book, the back of his shirt bulges out. FLUB notices this, knocks on the bulge. There is the sound of something solid. SNUB jerks away.)*

SNUB. Don't touch that!

FLUB. What is it?

SNUB. Nothing! It's none of your business! *(FLUB tries to get a good look at the bulge, but SNUB uses the prompt book to keep him at a distance.)* Stay back! I'm warning you! *(Keeping a watchful eye on FLUB, SNUB studies the prompt book.)* I'd have to say this is ... ahh—

STAGE MANAGER. Mackle! *(The STAGE MANAGER grabs the prompt book from SNUB. She returns SNUB and FLUB to their places.)* Go on!

FLUB. <Who ... ahh ... who will you marry this time, Father? I ask, although I am thrown slightly off balance by your sudden announcement.>

SNUB. <The woman who sold us the clock. With the red lipstick and the panty-line.>

STAGE MANAGER. A strange contortion flits across Flub's *mackle! (It does.)*

SNUB. <I am a little concerned now over your pending reaction—although not too much.>

FLUB *(menacingly).* <Ahh! The woman who sold us the clock!>

STAGE MANAGER. A Pinter silence. *(Silence. FLUB and SNUB square off.)*

FLUB. <I must admit, I feel a bit betrayed and hurt that you could arrive at such an important decision without first consulting me—your second but only living son.>

SNUB. <It couldn't be helped.>

STAGE MANAGER. Mackle grackle. *(Indeed.)*

FLUB. <Fortunately, I have news of my own, and this keeps me from losing my balance entirely. As you know, I have inherited your shifty and not entirely trustworthy disposition—along with your ravenous sexual desires. I, too, have decided to take a wife.>

SNUB. <I am feeling surprise.>

FLUB. <Good!>

SNUB. <A little shock...and yet pride that you—my second but only living son—find yourself comfortable speaking to me so openly about such intimate matters.>

FLUB. <Yes, well, as you know, you have raped me daily since my seventh birthday.>

SNUB. <Yes. That's true.>

FLUB. <So it is surprising that I would be this forthcoming. And yet I felt it necessary to inform you...I too am marrying the woman who sold us the clock. With the red lipstick and the panty-line.>

STAGE MANAGER *(presses the prompt book close to her face, scrunches her nose)*. Danger...danger...hangs on the...bear...like a...truffle. *(FLUB and SNUB exchange an awkward glance.)* The cook strikes three. *(Indeed, it does—the clock, that is. FLUB and SNUB exchange places.)*

FLUB. <Now I am really surprised.>

SNUB. <Flub Drubby Drub!>

FLUB. <A little angry at your insolence—although not too much, because of the guilt I feel over our sexual encounters—and yet happy in a strange sort of manic way.>

SNUB. <I'm glad we worked this out.>

FLUB. <As am I.>

STAGE MANAGER. Knockle tart.

SNUB *(to FLUB, after a concerned glance at the STAGE MANAGER).* <Well...as you know, I must to work within the hour—in the freezing blizzard—to hawk my wares. Although I don't really need to leave for another thirty minutes or so, I believe I will go now because of a rising fear that you may want to pork me if I stick around.>

FLUB. <You're very alert, son.>

SNUB. <Thank you. Goodbye, Father.>

FLUB. <Have a seat.>

SNUB. <Must I?>

FLUB. <Yes. Over here.> *(SNUB sits. FLUB puts a hand on his son's knee.)*

STAGE MANAGER. Snub in barging flittle snorkle gum. *(SNUB and FLUB steal another glance at the STAGE MANAGER. She sneezes. Then, all at once, FLUB is overcome with a spasm of understanding, a great rush of knowledge. He rises, transfixed, little gurgling sounds coming from his throat.)*

SNUB. What? *(More gurgling.)* What? What is it? What's wrong?

FLUB. At...at last!

SNUB. What?

FLUB. At last! I understand my role! I'm fleshing it out!

SNUB. Really?

FLUB. Yes! It's all clear to me now! His vision!

SNUB *(disbelief).* No!

FLUB. Yes!

SNUB. *Everything?*

FLUB. Yes!

SNUB. What about the clock?

FLUB. Yes!

SNUB. *The clock too?*

FLUB. Yes!

SNUB. My God!

FLUB. Yes!

SNUB *(to STAGE MANAGER).* A pen! Quick! Something to write with!

STAGE MANAGER. I...

SNUB. Hurry! Before he forgets!

STAGE MANAGER. I know there's...wait...I...I remember once...a long time ago...a...a truffle...a little chocolate bribe—

SNUB *(snatches a pen from her).* Paper!

STAGE MANAGER. I...I don't want to.

SNUB. *What?*

STAGE MANAGER. I don't want to anymore. You can't make me.

SNUB *(reaching for the prompt book).* Just tear a page from the—

STAGE MANAGER. No! *(She clutches the prompt book to her chest.)*

SNUB. This is no time for—

STAGE MANAGER *(terrified, a mother protecting her child).* No!

SNUB. Oh for crying out...fine! *(SNUB rushes to FLUB, offers him the pen, and holds out his other palm as a tablet.)* Here! Use my hand!

FLUB. What?

SNUB. My hand! I brought you a pen!

FLUB. Oh. Thank you. *(FLUB takes the pen and puts it in his pocket.)*

SNUB. What are you doing?

FLUB. Hmmm?

SNUB. The pen!

FLUB. What?

SNUB. The pen! I gave you a pen!

FLUB. Oh.

SNUB. Hurry! *(SNUB holds out his hand as a tablet.)*

FLUB. You know ... you really shouldn't give things away if you're not going to let people keep them. *(FLUB puts the pen in SNUB's outstretched palm.)*

SNUB. No! No! You had a revelation!

FLUB. A revelation?

SNUB. Yes!

FLUB. Did I?

SNUB. Yes! You were going to write it down for me! His vision! You said you'd figured it all out! Put it all together!

FLUB. *All of it?*

SNUB. Yes!

FLUB. What about the clock?

SNUB. Yes!

FLUB. *The clock too?*

SNUB. Yes!

FLUB. My God!

SNUB. Yes!

FLUB. I must have forgotten!

SNUB. Damn! *(SNUB flops down on the couch.)* I almost had it!

FLUB. Had what?

SNUB. Nothing. It's none of your business. *(Clock strikes nine. FLUB stands and moves to the opposite end of the couch. He sits. SNUB glares at the STAGE MANAGER as she prostrates herself in front of the clock, the prompt book still clutched to her chest. FLUB takes SNUB's hand and places it on his knee. Pause.)*

FLUB *(prompting SNUB).* "Don't be frightened, son." *(Pause. SNUB continues to glare at the STAGE MANAGER.)* "Don't be frightened, son."

SNUB *(reluctantly).* <Don't be frightened, son.>

FLUB. <I'm not, but what of our bride?>

SNUB. <Ah...*that.*>

FLUB. <The Gumbah.>

SNUB. <There's only one thing to do.> *(They thumb-wrestle.)*

STAGE MANAGER.
    His...
    his long arm
    dangling
    dangling
    rocking slightly
    tick
    tock
    tick
    tock

SNUB. <I win.>

FLUB. <You cheated! Your thumb is too long!>

SNUB. <It couldn't be helped.>

FLUB. <Two out of three!>

SNUB. <If you insist.> *(They thumb-wrestle.)*

STAGE MANAGER.
    his weight

I am not afraid
I am not afraid
I am not afraid
his long arm
dangling

(SNUB wins.)

FLUB. <It's monstrous! You're a freak! A mutant! Three out of five!>

STAGE MANAGER.
    pounding
    I am not afraid
    pounding

(FLUB loses.)

FLUB. <Four out of seven!>

STAGE MANAGER.
    down
    down
    down
    his long arm
    pounding
    my world
    changed
    rearranged
        with
            each

> fantastic
>
> blow

(FLUB loses again.)

FLUB. <Damn!>

STAGE MANAGER.
> my world
> the same
> rearranged
> always
> the
> same

FLUB. <There's no point to it! The cards are stacked!> *(The clock strikes one. The STAGE MANAGER panics at the sound of the clock. She dives under the table. SNUB and FLUB exchange places.)* <I am VICTORIOUS! Hah!> *(FLUB takes SNUB by the ear and leads him to the STAGE MANAGER.)* <Son, meet your mother. The woman who sold us the clock!>

SNUB. <Hello...Mother.>

STAGE MANAGER *(clinging to the table, terrified)*.
> mackle
> mackle grackle
> mackle grackle korpal fie *(Pause.)*

FLUB. What...what's wrong with her? *(SNUB kneels on the floor. FLUB follows.)* What is it? Is...is she all right? *(To STAGE MANAGER.)* Are you all right? *(No response.)* I think she's all right. She's just taking a breather.

SNUB *(to STAGE MANAGER).* Come here. *(She does not move.)* Come on. It's all right... I won't hurt you. *(SNUB reaches for her, but she lashes out violently.)*

STAGE MANAGER. Korpal fie! *(SNUB backs away. Pause.)*

SNUB. She's lost her mind.

FLUB. No ...

SNUB. It's the old man that did it! The bastard!

STAGE MANAGER *(to herself).*
    I am not afraid
    I am not afraid
    I am not afraid

SNUB. I warned her, but she wouldn't listen! I knew what he was after! What he wanted!

FLUB. It... it's just a little cold.

SNUB. I saw through him from the beginning! All of his *exercises!* His *rules!* He took advantage of her dedication! Of his position! He took advantage of us all! Corrupted us in his image!

FLUB *(continuing the play).* <She'll be a good mother!>

SNUB. WHAT?

FLUB. <She'll... she'll be a good mother.>

SNUB. How can you go on? LOOK AT HER! Look! Is that how you want to end up? Is it? Don't you see what he's doing? *(FLUB covers his ears.)* He wants to keep us eternally beneath him!

FLUB. I can't hear you!

SNUB. Idiot children forever worshiping at his feet!

FLUB. I'm completely deaf!

SNUB. Feeding his overgrown ego!

FLUB. You might as well be talking to a pole!

SNUB. As soon as we get comfortable in one role, we have to take on another! Why?

FLUB. <She'll be a good mother!>

SNUB. Because he wants to keep us off balance! That's why! Because he doesn't want us to THINK! He doesn't want us to QUESTION HIS AUTHORITY! So he keeps us busy! Keeps us running in circles! Like mice! Rushing from one role to the next! Well, I'm on to his game! I see what he's doing! And I refuse to participate! *(SNUB plants himself firmly on the couch. He folds his arms. FLUB looks around for a moment, panicked, then decides to play both roles.)*

FLUB *(as himself)*. <She'll be a good mother.> *(As SNUB.)* <In her fashion.> *(As himself.)* <She'll do the best she can.> *(As SNUB.)* <Will she tuck me in at night? And comfort me when I'm frightened? And feed me sugar plums? And read me stories until I fall asleep nestled between her breasts?> *(As himself.)* <Of course! Tell the boy a story!> *(FLUB pries the STAGE MANAGER from the table.)* Go on. *(He nudges her toward SNUB, but she keeps her distance, glaring suspiciously, half-crouched.)*

STAGE MANAGER. In...

FLUB. That's it.

STAGE MANAGER. In the...the...beginning...

FLUB. Ah! The old standard! Go on!

STAGE MANAGER. In...

FLUB. In the beginning...

STAGE MANAGER. In the beginning ... *(The STAGE MANAGER stands frozen, her eyes wide, ready to bolt at the slightest movement. Pause. FLUB turns to the audience.)*

FLUB. She tells it so well! She puts just the right emphasis! Go on! *(Pause.)* Go on.

STAGE MANAGER. In the beginning ... *(Another pause. She glares at SNUB suspiciously.)*

FLUB. In the beginning, everything was wonderful! Fine! OK, skip ahead! Let's have the juicy part! The climax!

STAGE MANAGER. In the ...

FLUB. The last ...

STAGE MANAGER *(agitated)*. The last ... days ...

FLUB. That's it!

STAGE MANAGER. The final ... hours ... the ... the clock ... struck ...

FLUB. Ah! The clock!

STAGE MANAGER. Struck ...

FLUB. The clock struck twelve!

STAGE MANAGER. His long arm ... pounding ...

FLUB. And then! What happened next? *(SNUB and the STAGE MANAGER glare at each other, motionless. Silence.)*

STAGE MANAGER. Nothing.

FLUB. N—*nothing?* *(A nervous little laugh.)* There must be *something!*

STAGE MANAGER *(staring deep into SNUB's soul)*. No. Darkness. *(SNUB glares back at her. The clock strikes four.)*

FLUB. Damn this eternal flip-flop!

STAGE MANAGER *(enraptured, prostrating herself in front of the clock)*. It's ... his vision!

SNUB. To hell with his vision!

FLUB. *What?*

SNUB. To hell with his vision! That's right! He isn't here to see it through! What about *our* vision?

FLUB. We...we don't have any vision! We're not allowed!

SNUB. Why not?

FLUB. Shhh! Not so—

SNUB. Not so loud? I hope he does hear!

FLUB. But he...he MADE you!

SNUB. And where is he NOW? *Huh?*

FLUB. You were NOTHING!

STAGE MANAGER (*childlike, an exploration of her own little world*). Clay...

FLUB. An unknown!

STAGE MANAGER. Dirt...

FLUB. He taught you everything! Took you under his wing! Educated you!

SNUB. Hah!

FLUB. You were like a son to him!

STAGE MANAGER. Sand...

SNUB. And when it comes down to the wire, he's nowhere to be found—is he? Vanished into thin air! The great director!

STAGE MANAGER (*feeling her stomach*). Lumpy...

FLUB. Without him, you're lost! You're nothing! A second-rate actor! A child!

STAGE MANAGER. A...

SNUB. I AM NOT A CHILD!

STAGE MANAGER. A child...

FLUB. The best you can do is follow! Blindly! You can't grasp it! You can't get your mind around it!

STAGE MANAGER (*feeling her belly. A grand discovery*). A child!

FLUB. It's beyond you!

STAGE MANAGER. Oh! A clay baby! (*The STAGE MANAGER rubs her belly, delighted. A soft little laugh. SNUB and FLUB watch, dumbstruck.*)

FLUB. She...she's not... (*The STAGE MANAGER grabs her belly, feeling a little kick for the first time.*)

STAGE MANAGER. Oh!

FLUB. No! She...she can't be! He couldn't have! Could he? He...he's beyond that!

SNUB. The bastard!

FLUB. He...he must have had some reason! Some purpose! A...a greater plan!

SNUB. Hah!

FLUB. Everything happens for a reason! It's not our place to question! It will all come clear in the end!

STAGE MANAGER.

    In me
    there is order
    in my body
    meaning
    I hold the secret
    here
    traces
    left behind
    fragments
    shadows
    fill in the blank
    I am a rune
    a carrot

a little joke
I am the Moon
No man can ever know
never know me
possess me

SNUB. But I have.

STAGE MANAGER. You haven't.

SNUB. I have! I've known you!

STAGE MANAGER. No...you only thought you had!

SNUB. Listen to me! Listen! Your...your mind is clouded right now. OK? You're not thinking clearly. We have to get away from here. That's all. Away from *him!* And then everything will fall back into place! Like a dream! Like...like waking up and finding what's real! *(Pause.)* I found an old play. *(He pulls a very old, cloth-covered book from his shirt.)* It's one you've never read. It was supposed to have been burned years ago—along with all of its kind—it didn't fit the director's vision. But somehow...it survived! An original copy! I found it in an old bookstore! They didn't know what they had! I... I was waiting to give it to you...waiting for just the right moment...but now...now I...here. *(He offers her the book. She glares at him.)* Please...please take it. *(Pause.) Please? (Pause.)* We'll...we'll read it together. OK? It will open your eyes to a...a whole new world! A whole new language of the stage! A forgotten language! We'll...we'll talk about what it means...about... about our real feelings. We'll have meaningful discussions. And...and one day...we'll wake up...and everything will be just...just like it used to be. *(The STAGE MANAGER takes the book from SNUB. Sniffs it.)*

STAGE MANAGER. A truffle.

SNUB. What? No...

STAGE MANAGER. A little chocolate bribe.

SNUB. No. That...that was a long time ago. *(Pause.)* Am I never to be forgiven? Am I to be eternally punished for one little indiscretion? One childish blunder?

STAGE MANAGER. Always the same.

SNUB. No! No, not always the same! Not always the same! I've served my penance! I've done everything I could to make up for it! Suffered countless humiliations. Groveled at your feet! What more do you want from me? Haven't I suffered enough? *(Pause.)* I can save you. *(Pause.)* Are you willing to sacrifice your own happiness just to spite me? *(She drops the book. SNUB picks it up.)* Don't...don't do this. Listen. Listen to me. He was a false prophet. You have to wipe him out of your— *(He reaches for her.)*

STAGE MANAGER *(violently).* Korpal fie! *(SNUB rises. Backs away. She sneezes. Wipes her nose. Sneezes again. Rubs her belly. A soft, little laugh. Silence. SNUB tosses the old book to the ground. He picks up one of the chairs and smashes it to the ground as well, breaking it into pieces. He picks up a jagged, heavy piece of wood. Brandishes it.)*

FLUB. What...what are you doing?

SNUB. He's taken her away from me! Brainwashed her completely! *(FLUB throws himself in front of the STAGE MANAGER.)*

FLUB. Stay back! I'm warning you! *(SNUB takes a step towards them.)*

SNUB. *What?*

FLUB. Stay away from her! I...I won't allow it!

SNUB. Not her.

FLUB *(uneasily)*. Not...not her?

SNUB. No. *(Pause. FLUB throws himself in front of the clock.)*

FLUB. Don't come any closer!

SNUB. Get out of the way.

FLUB. Perhaps...perhaps he will return!

SNUB. No.

FLUB. Perhaps he's on his way! This very moment! Perhaps he's here! Let's have a look! *(FLUB drags SNUB to the edge of the stage.)*

SNUB. Let go of me! *(FLUB peers into the audience. Examines each face.)*

FLUB. No. No. No. No. No.

SNUB. You're wasting your time!

FLUB. No. No. No. No.

SNUB. He isn't coming back!

FLUB. No. No. No.

SNUB. Perhaps he's dead already! Did you think of that?

FLUB. No!

SNUB. And if he *does* show his face, I'll break it in two! I'll smash his brains in! *(FLUB spots something in the auditorium. He stares hard.)*

FLUB. Is that...there...in the...it's him!

SNUB. *What?*

FLUB. It's him! It's him! He's come back! He's returned! At last! We're saved! *(SNUB steps forward, brandishing his weapon.)*

SNUB. *Where?*

STAGE MANAGER. At last!

FLUB. There!

SNUB. Where?

FLUB. There!

STAGE MANAGER. At last!

SNUB. I can't see!

FLUB. There! In the last row!

SNUB. The last row?

FLUB. We're saved!

SNUB. There?

FLUB. Yes!

SNUB. *Right there?*

FLUB. Yes! *(SNUB peers into the audience.)*

SNUB. It isn't him.

FLUB. It is!

SNUB. No.

FLUB. Shut up! You're insane!

SNUB *(bitterly).* Ask *her* if you don't believe me! She ought to know! *(The STAGE MANAGER sneezes.)*

FLUB *(to STAGE MANAGER).* Well? *(FLUB leads the STAGE MANAGER to the front of the stage. There is a long, hopeful silence as she stares into the audience. The clock strikes twelve. After a moment, she lowers her head and turns away.)* Well? *(Pause.)* Did you see him or didn't you? *(Pause.)* Didn't you? *(The STAGE MANAGER grows agitated, begins to moan softly.)* What? What is it? What's wrong?

SNUB. It...it's stopped.

FLUB. What? *(SNUB points to the clock. Its pendulum stands still. There is only silence.)* It's... *(He approaches the clock. Touches it.)* It's...no...no, it can't... *(To SNUB.)* What have you done?

SNUB. I didn't touch it.

FLUB. It can't be! *(FLUB tries to set the pendulum in motion. At his touch, however, the clock collapses.*

Falls to pieces.) What... what does this mean? What does it mean? I don't... I don't understand! *(FLUB tries desperately to rebuild the clock, but only makes things worse.)* No! How... how could he leave us? Now! When we need him most! He... he said he'd always be here! Until the end of time! He... *(FLUB turns to the clock, terrified.)* ... he promised. *(Pause.)* And now... he's... it's all... it's all falling apart... and he's not... he's not here to... to put it all... *(Pause.)* WHERE IS HE? *(Pause.)* He must... he must be on his way! He's been held up! That's all! Caught in traffic! The streets are empty, I admit, but... all of those lights... some of them still work, and he's... he's probably... oh wait... I've got it! He's found another theatre! That's it! A new space! And he wanted to surprise us! Oh, how exciting! We've been acting like such babies! He'll have a good laugh at our expense, won't he? I can't wait to see! A new stage! It must be something wonderful! Not like this one! This husk! No! This is only a shadow! A mustard seed! Why it's... it's probably beyond our ability to grasp! Something magnificent for once! A... a single site! With no partition! No barrier! No auditorium! *(FLUB jumps down from the stage and into the audience.)* One space! All of us together! A hundred thousand swiveling seats! Always a full house! And lots of clapping! Clapping and laughter! And... and lights! Oh! Lights! All kinds of luminous vibrations! Fresnels of gold shooting light in waves, in sheets, in fusillades of fiery arrows! A living theatre! It's going to be something! He must be on his way! Right now! To tell us! To let us know! I'm going to tell him all of the silly ideas we've passed around! We'll all have a good laugh! All of us! A nice little chuckle! He's...he's probably at the door right now! There! That cough! Did you hear it? I'd know that cough anywhere! We have to give him a great welcome! *(FLUB throws open the doors of the theatre, but there is no one there. Pause.)* I...I don't...

STAGE MANAGER *(to herself)*. Alone. *(She lies on the floor and begins to babble nonsense as she rocks back and forth. SNUB stands over her as FLUB makes his way back to the stage. Silence.)*

FLUB. I've...I've made a great fool of myself. Haven't I?

SNUB. It doesn't matter. *(Pause.)*

FLUB. What...ahh...what...what happens now?

SNUB. Now? *(Pause.)* Nothing. Darkness. *(SNUB pulls a cigarette from his pocket. Lights it.)*

FLUB. How...how can you be sure?

SNUB. I'm sure. *(A deep drag.)* We're free at last.

FLUB. Free?

SNUB. That's right. *(Pause.)* Our penance is over. *(Silence.)*

FLUB. What...what's that.

SNUB. What?

FLUB. That. Listen. *(The sound of a clock can be heard ticking ever so faintly.)*

SNUB. Echoes.

FLUB. No... *(FLUB examines the remains of the clock, but they are silent. The ticking grows louder. FLUB begins to circle the stage. Gradually, he zeros in on the STAGE MANAGER. He circles her. Puts an ear to her belly. His eyes grow wide.)* My God!

SNUB. What?

FLUB. Listen! *(SNUB does not move.)*

SNUB. What?

FLUB. Go on! *(SNUB does not budge.)*

SNUB. It can't be.

FLUB. It is!

SNUB. But—

FLUB. Listen! *(Still, SNUB does not move.)*

SNUB. It...it wouldn't make any sense.

FLUB. I'm telling you! *(The ticking grows louder. The STAGE MANAGER giggles as FLUB pokes her belly.)* It's a miracle! I knew he'd make arrangements!

SNUB. It can't be! There's...there's no logical explanation!

FLUB. So what! Mackle grackle! *(FLUB begins to hop madly about the stage, clapping wildly.)* Mackle grackle korpal fie! Korpal fie! Korpal fie!

SNUB. She...she can't have a *clock* inside her! What kind of sense would that make? It's ridiculous! *(The STAGE MANAGER grabs her belly—another kick.)*

STAGE MANAGER. Oh!

FLUB. We'll...we'll raise it as our own! A wolf cub! A... a child of the theatre!

SNUB. *What?*

FLUB. Someone has to take responsibility! The director's gone, and...and she's near the end. I'm sorry, but it's true. You might as well face up to it. She doesn't have much time left. We'll have to watch her so she doesn't wander off. This is going to be exciting! A real adventure! I'll...I'll nurture the child! Comfort it! Generations will call me blessed!

SNUB. You?

FLUB. Yes!

SNUB. What kind of father would *you* make?

The Father Clock 239

FLUB. Do you have a better idea? *(FLUB puts a hand on the STAGE MANAGER's belly.)* Stub. I call you Stub because that is your name. Stub Drub.

SNUB. Are you blind? It's another trick! That's all it is! Another illusion to distract you! *(The STAGE MANAGER cries out. This time, however, she grabs her stomach in pain.)*

STAGE MANAGER. Oh! *(She freezes, startled by the pain. Long pause. Finally, fear in her eyes, she turns to FLUB.)*

FLUB. It... it's trying to tell us something!

SNUB. The *clock-thing?* The *mutant?*

FLUB. Yes! Maybe—

STAGE MANAGER *(clearly in pain)*. Oh!

FLUB. My God! It... it's coming!

SNUB. *What?*

FLUB. It's coming! The child is coming!

STAGE MANAGER. The child!

SNUB. It can't be!

FLUB. Yes! The child!

STAGE MANAGER. The child!

SNUB. Look, whatever that... that *thing* is... it's not a child! Don't let it fool you! It's been around forever! Since the beginning of time! In some deep, dark hole somewhere! Some chasm! Just waiting for some poor fool like you to come along and set it free! *(The STAGE MANAGER grimaces, her pains growing stronger.)*

STAGE MANAGER. Oh!

SNUB. It's going to grow into another tyrant! You know that! Some great beast trampling everything in its path!

STAGE MANAGER. In... in me there is order!

FLUB. Yes!

SNUB. Another Caesar! Or worse!

FLUB. Order!

SNUB. I won't allow it!

STAGE MANAGER. In my body!

FLUB. That's right!

SNUB. I can't!

STAGE MANAGER. Meaning!

SNUB. I'll fight it till the end! *(Once again, FLUB is overcome with a sudden rush of knowledge, little gurgling sounds come up out of his throat. He gestures wildly at SNUB, horrified.)* What? What is it?

FLUB. I...I know you!

SNUB. Of course you know me.

FLUB. No! I...I know you! I know who you are! I see through your disguise!

SNUB. My *disguise?*

FLUB. Yes! *(Pause.)*

SNUB. You've known me since I was a child. *(FLUB grabs a piece of wood from the broken chair and brandishes it.)* What's gotten into you?

FLUB. Stay back!

SNUB. What?

FLUB. Stay away from her! All right. Look. Why don't you just sit down for a minute? OK? Sit down. Take a deep breath. Try to relax. And let me take care of this. Don't come any closer! I'm warning you! *(FLUB lunges at SNUB, brandishing his weapon. The STAGE MANAGER cries out in pain.)*

SNUB. She needs help!

FLUB. I'll help her! *(FLUB kneels beside the STAGE MANAGER.)* Breathe. *(She does.)* That's it. Take my hand. *(She takes his hand and squeezes hard as she cries out.)* OK. That's it. OK. OK, not *quite* so hard. *(The STAGE MANAGER cries out.)* I...I see a...a foot! No...something...not a foot, but a...a...a shoulder perhaps? Or a knee? Maybe a very small bottom? Something with a little curve to it... *(The STAGE MANAGER cries out.)* Push! *(Again, the STAGE MANAGER cries out.)* What? What's wrong? What is it? Are you in pain? Here! Squeeze my hand! *(She begins to sob.).* What? Is something wrong? *(Pause.)* Oh God...oh God...it's...I...I think it's...it's stuck! The...the child is stuck! What do we do now? I don't want to hurt her! Breathe! I...I didn't expect complications! *(FLUB retrieves the prompt book. Flips through it, desperately searching for instructions of some sort.)* I...I don't...I don't know what to do! *(Another cry.)* Oh God, she's in pain! Help me! *(SNUB laughs, delighted. He takes the prompt book from FLUB.)*

SNUB. Very good! *(SNUB applauds.)*

FLUB. *What?*

SNUB. Very good. That's a nice moment.

FLUB. How can you—

SNUB *(scribbling something in the prompt book).* OK... take five.

FLUB. *What?*

SNUB. Take five. *(Pause.)* It's the final step. The only logical conclusion. *(SNUB exits, still scribbling, his mind racing, the cigarette dangling from his lips. FLUB looks a little befuddled.)*

FLUB. What...ahh...what...what did he mean by that? That last remark? *(The STAGE MANAGER cries out. FLUB tries to comfort her.)*

STAGE MANAGER. I am a carrot!

FLUB. Yes.

STAGE MANAGER. A little joke! *(She bursts into hysterical laughter which degenerates into a long, painful sob. FLUB holds his head as if it might explode, begins to scurry about the stage like a mouse.)*

FLUB. He...he's really quite fond of the clock! He's confided in me many times just how...how fond of it he is! How it comforts him! Nurtures him! Suckles him like a— *(The STAGE MANAGER cries out, much louder than before. FLUB is drawn to her, cringing. He pauses.)* It's... *(Again, she cries out. FLUB moves closer.)* It's...it's coming! It's coming! Isn't it? *(She nods through the pain.)* My God! It's coming! Push! That's it! I...I can't believe it's...it's really— *(She cries out.)* Good! That's it! Almost there! We're getting closer! One! Last! *(One great final scream. The STAGE MANAGER collapses from exhaustion. FLUB rises from between the STAGE MANAGER's legs. In his hands he holds a ringing alarm clock.)* ...time. *(As the lights begin their final fade to black, they linger for a moment on FLUB. Alone. With his clock. Ringing into the darkness.)*

END